GREEN DAY

UNCENSORED

ON THE RECORD

By Tom King

C⬤DA
BOOKS LTD

C⊕DA
BOOKS LTD

www.codabooks.com

This edition is published in Great Britain in 2012 by

Coda Books Ltd., Office Suite 2, Shrieves Walk, 39 Sheep Street, Stratford-upon-Avon, Warwickshire CV37 6GJ

www.codabooks.com

The Green Day Phenomenon illustrations by Cristy Road.

Photographs courtesy of Pictorial Press, Rex Features and PA Photos.

A CIP catalogue record for this book is available from the British Library.

ISBN: 978-1-78158-245-9

MUSIC REVIEWS LTD

CONTENTS

INTRODUCTION

In 2006, punk is alive and well – and even flourishing. While the spirit of rebellion that fuelled the original movement of 1976 has been diffused (and, some say, defused) by today's slacker generation, if it's power and aggression you're looking for, you need look no further than the wave of American punk bands that have penetrated today's mainstream. While esteemed acts such as The Offspring and Rancid are bearing the flag for intelligent rebel music, they're a long way behind the most successful band of all – Green Day – whose stratospheric rise to the top of the rock tree has been both rapid and unexpected.

The story of Green Day is one of a rise, a fall and a spectacular rebirth, after a decade in the spotlight and a career that had seen as many fans drop away as had signed up to the cause. The text that follows explores the roots of singer/ guitarist Billie Joe Armstrong, bassist Mike Dirnt and drummer Tre Cool from their unsavoury roots on San Francisco's East Bay punk scene, through to their explosion into the wider public consciousness with 1994's Dookie and the subsequent turbulent decade. In 2004 they defied all critics with their career-high album American Idiot, a concept album (whisper the term!) that redefined the pop-punk genre and staked their highly arguable claim as biggest band in the world for all to see.

Enjoy the ride in all its technicolour glory.

Tom King, 2006

THE GREEN DAY PHENOMENON

BY: CRISTY C. ROAD

DUDE, WHATEVER WE ARE PLAYING *DOES NOT* SOUND LIKE *METALLICA!*

DEEP IN THE HOLLOW TRENCHES OF *RODEO, CA* TWO TEENAGE METALHEADS, *BILLIE JOE AND MIKE*, COMBINED FORCES TO START A BAND, *SWEET CHILDREN*, IN THE LATE 1980S.

EVENTUALLY, *SWEET CHILDREN* FOUND A DRUMMER NAMED JOHN, CHANGED THEIR NAME TO *GREEN DAY*, AND STARTED PLAYING SHOWS AT 924 *GILMAN ST.*- THE LOCAL HAVEN OF THE *BERKELEY, CA* PUNK CIRCUIT.

GILMAN ST.

AROUND 1991, JOHN LEFT THE BAND AND WAS REPLACED WITH *TRE COOL*- A MENDOCINO NATIVE, DRUMMER OF THE *LOOKOUTS*, AND WEARER OF DRESSES. SOON AFER, *GREEN DAY* WENT TO RECORD A 2ND ALBUM WITH *LOOKOUT* RECORDS AND FANS *FLOODED* SHOWS MORE EACH DAY.

CONTINUED ON PAGE 70...

THE STORY OF GREEN DAY

In 1972, when three kids called Billie, Mike and Frank were born in California, punk was still four years from its own birth, although the term itself existed with various meanings. But the urgent strain of anger and frustration that typified the music was there, all right – ingrained in the fabric of society, especially in the difficult childhoods of the kids that would later grow up to embrace it. Got a theory about the roots of the third wave of punk? Try this one on for size...

The town of Rodeo, a small fish in the big sea of California, is close to the college settlement of Berkeley, although geographic proximity is just about all it has in common with one of America's best-known intellectual hotbeds. A quiet, unassuming place, Rodeo was entirely unmoved by the arrival on 17 February 1972 of Billie Joe Armstrong, the son of a truck driver (and occasional jazz musician) father, and a mother who worked as a waitress at a restaurant called Rod's Hickory Pit and liked listening to country and western. Along with his five siblings, Billie Joe was neither destined for material wealth nor academic success – and so, even from his earliest days, he tried to carve out a niche for himself in other, less orthodox ways. As a schoolkid he would spend much time on juvenile pranks on his teachers and his fellow students, such as allowing other runners to lap him on the athletics track before racing in at the final straight to make onlookers think that he'd won. He also tried his hardest to attract girls, with mixed success: as he later said, "School is practice for the future, practice makes perfect, and nobody's perfect... so why practise?"

However, signs of the nascent punk within Armstrong began to emerge after his father died of cancer and his mother was left with six children to support. After she remarried, he often got into scuffles with his stepfather, and this aggression against authority was carried over into other areas of his life. Like so many other children with similar problems, Billie Joe turned to music for support, and began to study the guitar and sing songs: this was helped by the talent he had been showing as a musician since an early age: believe it or not, he was reportedly singing tunes at the age of two, had begun entertaining local hospital patients at five years old and had even recorded a home-made single entitled 'Looking For Love' at the Fiat record company. An early musical eye-opener for Billie was The Replacements' Sorry Ma, Forgot to Take Out the Trash, introduced to him by his sister Anna (who beat him up after he scratched it). His late father had bought him a Fernandes guitar – which soon became Armstrong's constant companion – and he devoted himself to mastering it. By the age of 15, he was playing in a band called Sweet Children with a bass-playing friend called Mike Dirnt.

Dirnt, born Michael Pritchard on 4 May 1972, had to endure the misfortune of having a mother who was addicted to heroin. Needless to say, her parenting skills weren't great. As he recalled, "When I was in fourth or fifth grade, my mom stayed out all night, came home the next day with a guy, and then he moved in. I'd never met the guy before, and all of a sudden he's my stepdad." Once, when his mother attempted to play the role of parent with obvious reluctance, he reacted. "I took my mom aside," he explained, "and I said to her, 'This is how it is. You have so much shit going on in your life, so if once every semester you ask me if I've done my homework and jump all over my case, that's not right. Have I failed yet? No. And I'm going to graduate if you stay off my back. The one time in your life you choose to have morals, and it's going to fuck me up. Don't play mom once a year. It doesn't fucking cut it.'"

He added, "Later on, when I hit high school, my mom moved away from us, and my stepdad and me got real close.

He instilled a lot in me. The one thing my family did give me is blue-collar morals. But then he died when I was 17... Life is full of challenges. You just have stare them straight in the eye and walk forward."

Mike was adopted by a Native American foster mother and a white father. However, the couple divorced when he was seven, and he was passed from family to family for several years. After a stint back with his birth mother in his early teens, Mike spent time living in a truck before finally moving into his own apartment, attached to the house belonging to his schoolfriend Billie Joe Armstrong's family. Striking up a friendship with Billie Joe and taking up the bass guitar, Mike settled down for a while, but was plagued by a heart problem (making him prone to panic attacks) and hyperactivity, which made him the target of bullying at school. Still, like Billie he was devoted to punk rock and the pair would make regular trips to the record shops

of Berkeley to acquire albums from classic punk artists such as the Sex Pistols and the Ramones.

Mike's entrée into bass was less than glamorous, as he recalled. "My first bass was a pawnshop bass and had two flatwound strings, an E and an A. My mom got it. It was a total piece of shit, it was a generic 60s bass with buttons on it. Then I got a job and saved $200 for a Peavey. I then played a Gibson Grabber 3 with three pickups – I had to buy the G3 after I dropped the Peavey and it broke in half. The guy sold it to me for $180 and then heard how good it sounded and went, damn! I played that for about 700 shows. Then I broke the neck again..."

The key bass players in his life were the punk and classic rock giants: "When I was a kid I really liked Tommy Stinson of The Replacements, and I was always a big fan of Paul McCartney. Even though I don't play like him I try to think like him, just to be tasteful on the bass. The simplicity of it is amazing. Very bluesy and jazzy in the same line. John McVie, too – even though Fleetwood Mac is a guilty pleasure, all their songs have great bass-lines. And Cliff Burton of Metallica of course, I really loved his aggression... Paul Simenon, of course. I really respected what a great reggae player he was. 'Rock The Casbah' has an awesome bass line – listen to the way it goes higher! But nowadays I'm trying to think a bit like the modern English kind of playing, like Radiohead or maybe Coldplay. Totally in the pocket, and it really warms everything up. Like Husker Dü. You're playing and then you're not playing, and you're leaving pockets of air. I do play chords but I'm always careful not to overplay – sometimes I do some stuff that I realise is a little overkill. But I have my hands full playing live!"

"If you wanted to hear music in our town, you had to play it," Mike later told Rip magazine. "We didn't have a record store in town. We were little kids. Our parents were counting every dime, you know? But over time, we saved up ourselves and Billie got a guitar and played stuff. Then I started saving like crazy while I learnt to play guitar, and then I finally got one. Billie and me jammed together and with other people. We tried different bands and played in, like, talent shows at school and stuff. Then all of a sudden we got introduced to punk music and it was the coolest freakin' thing. I mean, here we are playing loud music on junky amps and everything, and that's exactly what those bands were doing. It wasn't so much how they influenced us, it just kept us energised."

Inevitably the two teenagers formed a band (Billie Joe would later describe early rehearsals in his garage as 'our version of bad heavy metal'; songs they 'perfected' include 'Ain't Talking About Love' by Van Halen, 'Photograph' by Def Leppard and 'Crazy Train' by Ozzy Osbourne) and, hooking in a drummer named John Kiffmeyer (whose stage name was Al Sobrante, after his hometown of El Sobrante), began to assemble a live set. All they needed now was somewhere to play – but Kiffmeyer, who was connected to a few local promoters through the moderate success of his previous band, Isocracy, knew the man to speak to.

Enter a local musician, promoter and all-round punk activist Lawrence Livermore, who was in the process of setting up a punk club in the East Bay area of San Francisco (a run-down but musically active area where bands such as Metallica were evolving at around the same time). Livermore was playing at the time in a band called The Lookouts, whose name he had taken for his backroom record label Lookout and who consisted of himself on guitar and vocals, a bassist and a kid drummer called Frank Edwin Wright III. The last of these – born on 9 December, 1972, and a mere 12 years old when Livermore recruited him into his band back in 1984 – had been born in Frankfurt, Germany, but grew up in the Mendocino mountains

of North California, a logging, fishing and wine-growing region of immense natural beauty. "We lived about an hour from the nearest town," Wright said later, "and the only contact we had with the outside world was from this little grey boom box with one radio station, a kind of pop-rock deal. Hall & Oates, Huey Lewis, all that shit." Wright's dad was a retired Vietnam helicopter pilot who had built many of the houses in the area, including the one belonging to Livermore: Lawrence gave Frank a drum lesson and then renamed him Tre Cool when he joined the band. "You need a punk name if you're going to be in a punk band," Livermore told him. "From now on you're Tre Cool." "I used to play with the older dudes, grey-haired guys," Tre later recalled, "and I was this little shithead who was like, 'yeah, yeah, let me hit something'."

As Tre recalled of his early career: "I started out playing punk rock when I was 11 years old. That's when I was in my first band The Lookouts. The other guys were 38 and 16, and they were just going in to make their first album. They needed a drummer pretty bad, because the last one had moved to Brazil and the guitarist kept her drums. I was like, 'hey, let me try out!' So immediately, the guitarist takes away my cymbals because I was bashing and thrashing them. I had to play a lot of fast punk rock right away. That was the beginning of my drumming days. I went home and told my Dad, 'Yeah, I'm going to be a drummer'. He said, 'Well, if you can rub your stomach at the same time as you pat your head, at the same time as you're jumping up and down on one leg and kicking the other one out in a circle... and saying 'The Pledge of Allegiance...' I did all that just like, bam, you know."

"Drums started to be the only thing I was excited about," he added. "School sucked. I was a bad student. Too rambunctious, and I never paid attention. But I thought bands were cool. I was totally into the idea of being in a band. I liked how bands looked at the award shows in their little sparkle suits. I wanted to practise real hard and get to that level. When you're a little kid, that stuff looks pretty rocking and impressive... I didn't know what I was doing, but they were playing punk songs and I just started keeping the beat. From that point on I was always playing punk and trying to get faster and tighter and better."

"I wanted to be like the guy from Duran Duran," he went on. "I was listening to punk all day and so I really started paying attention to what the drummers were doing. I didn't get my own set until my dad sprung for a Pearl kit for my thirteenth birthday, but then I got headphones and a Walkman and started playing along to The Cars, Zeppelin and AC/DC – playing along to AC/DC is the best way to learn how to play rock! They're the easiest drum parts ever, and they make you feel like you're king of the world almost right away!"

The Lookouts went on to record some obscure 7" singles and an album – now hard to find and as a result highly collectable – and by 1986 Livermore had set up the renowned Gilman Street Project, a punk club where bands played according to a strict all-ages, no alcohol, no rock-star-posing-allowed policy and where the musicians mingled freely with the crowds. Soon a hardcore punk ethic developed, barring any band who had signed to a major label from playing there, ensuring that the venue's underground credentials remained intact. On the flipside of this integrity-first approach, of course, was the fact that the Gilman Street scene was forever destined to remain unexposed and undeveloped. An early band to perform there was Sweet Children – Armstrong, Dirnt and Kiffmeyer – who had been highly impressed by another influential punk act that played there, Operation Ivy, who had married pop choruses with punk riffage.

In 1987 Tre asked Livermore if The Lookouts could play a set in the backwoods of their Mendocino mountain home, near where both men lived. "Some kids at my school are having a party this Friday night," he told Livermore. "Can The Lookouts play?" Delighted to have an opportunity to perform without the long slog down from the mountains into San Francisco, Livermore agreed. Shortly after he received a phone call from Kiffmeyer, who was looking for possible gigs for Sweet Children. Livermore recalled Isocracy's chaotic shows (they were known for their habit of bringing bags of rubbish on stage and throwing it at the audience) and was keen to help out, even though all he had to offer was the forthcoming Mendocino forest gig. As Livermore recalled to Metal Hammer in 2005, Kiffmeyer told him, "I'm in a new band with these two kids from Rodeo. We're called Sweet Children, and I was wondering if you knew any shows we could play." "Not much going on right now," was the answer. "The only show we've got coming up is this high school party that Tre set up for us... it'd be a 280-mile round trip for you guys, it's up in the mountains, it's supposed to snow, we don't even know if anybody will show up. And there's no money for the bands, not even for gas."

But Kiffmeyer was keen, and the legendary Sweet Children/Lookouts 'date' duly took place. As Livermore recalled, "The 'party' was a total fiasco. When we got there, five kids were standing around freezing outside an old wooden cabin. Nobody had a key, so we had to break in. There was no heat except for a wood stove, no light except for candles, and no electricity until we brought in a generator to power the amps."

After this inauspicious start, Sweet Children, The Lookouts and the other bands on the East Bay punk scene – as Livermore described them, "kids who never even thought about being in a band [who] saw their friends and schoolmates up on stage and thought, 'If they can do that, why can't I?' Half of them were still in high school..." – focused their attentions, short as most of them may have been, on the Gilman Street club and its attendant scene. Luckily for Armstrong and Dirnt, Livermore had been impressed enough by the mountain gig to offer them a record deal on his tiny label. By 1989 he had booked them into a studio to record four songs for a debut EP titled 1,000 Hours.

Two weeks before the EP's release, the band told Livermore they were changing their name to Green Day, inspired by a heavy day of dope-smoking. ("A Green Day is a day with lots of green bud where you just sit around taking bong hits, hanging around" said Mike, helpfully.) The response: "What, are you crazy? You can't change your name at the last minute! How will anybody know it's you? Besides, Green Day's a stupid name. It doesn't even mean anything." But the band were resolute, and a new EP sleeve was duly designed. The EP came out in April '89 and sold about 1000 copies in its first year, not even matching up the Lookout label's best seller to date, a record from Operation Ivy.

Things moved fast. Livermore later put up the grand total of $675 for the band to record a full album, 39/Smooth, which was made over two days, mostly of first takes. This vinyl LP was later reissued on CD as 1,039 Smoothed Out Slappy Hours with the addition of tracks from the 1,000 Hours and Slappy EPs (the latter was recorded in 1990) plus the track 'I Want To Be Alone', taken from a compilation album called The Big One. The album's rawness was its charm: "I look back at 39/Smooth," said Billie Joe Armstrong in 2004, "and I honestly think that we would have fucked it up had we had more time or more money to do it differently."

Green Day's first US tour set off the day after Mike graduated from high school, a 45-concert jaunt on which the band were full of enthusiasm but which was full of organisational nightmares. The first show in Arcata took place in the living room of a fan's apartment, as no proper venue had been organised for them to play in. Slappy was recorded during a stopover in Minneapolis and, despite van breakdowns, show cancellations and unscrupulous

promoters, the trio of Armstrong, Dirnt and Kiffmeyer loved it. On their return to Berkeley, it became apparent that the tour had attracted a kind of fanbase for them, with shows aplenty coming their way and the debut LP selling well. However, a bombshell awaited in the form of Kiffmeyer, who departed without much notice, even though it later emerged that he had been planning to attend college in Arcata for a couple of years. Armstrong only heard the news through a mutual friend, and was depressed by it, as he told Livermore: "It blew me away," he said, "I was hurt. One, because I had to hear it from someone else, but also because John was a big influence to us. We were so young, and he's a really smart person. We learned a lot from him."

Billie didn't like Kiffmeyer's suggestion that he and Dirnt should put Green Day on hold until he returned from college: "We were way too young and full of energy to wait six months or a year for someone to play gigs," he said. "At 18, that's like half a lifetime. At the same time, I had this romantic thing about how the gang doesn't split up, the band doesn't split up. I didn't want to look for another member, it was too cheesy, too lame." Besides, Billie had made the band his life: he had dropped out of high school the day before his eighteenth birthday.

Billie Joe recalled: "I kind of moved out of my house and did a couch tour of friends' homes, different places. Then I started a band in 1988. I was 15. I was only five years old when [the first wave of punk] came out, I was too young to witness it. I got more into late-80s punk bands like Social Distortion."

Fortunately, an appropriate replacement was at hand in the form of Tre Cool, now 18 like Billie and Mike and raring to go. Armstrong already knew him – he had recorded guest guitar and vocals on The Lookouts' recent LP – and early jam sessions with the new line-up in autumn 1990 proved fruitful. "I was excited to see how well Tre blended in with the band," recalled Livermore later, "but sad, too, because I knew it probably meant the end of The Lookouts. Tre didn't become a full-fledged member right away. John was still coming back to play some gigs, but he was also playing with another band at college."

"Al [aka John] also encouraged us to play with Tre," explained Mike Dirnt much further down the line. "We always joked that it was a bit like saying, look, I'm not going to be around for a while, so why don't you fuck this other guy while I'm gone. He's much better in bed than me!"

Of Kiffmeyer, Tre once explained: "I was friends with their drummer, though he was way older than me. He's left-handed and he played all goofy, with the kick drum on the right and side cymbal on the left. He used to make these wonderful, cool mistakes. Playing these beats where it sounded like you're falling downstairs."

Tre is, many affirm, the very picture of a walking punk timebomb. When he says, "Shit happens, man. You get gasoline, you fuck around with it a little bit, it goes all over your face – before you know it, your head is on fire", you know it comes from personal experience. In fact, he experiments from time to time with firebreathing – as he once recalled, "I was shooting fire out of my mouth! So far, I've managed to make it to 30 feet. This one time I'd had too much fuel and not enough air, so it shot back and my mouth exploded. I looked like Freddie Krueger! It was fucking cool, dude!"

"I've been on fire four times," he adds, "and I've been on fire twice on stage. I've been hospitalised many times. My hands are like leather, which is pretty cool. I've had therapists yelling at me for not taking better care of my body. I'm like a sack of potatoes to be abused at will."

Adding, "I want to be one of those people that dogs find buried under a ton of snow – almost dying of starvation", he lists, "Fisher Price music, nursery rhymes, and the alphabet song" as his influences. "Rock and roll needs to come back to the days of Keith Moon and The Who," he told Modern Drummer. "Just causing trouble. Causing shit. That's our role now. We're the ones making trouble, canning the most damage of any other band. We have the power right now to do anything we want."

Powered up by their new drummer, Green Day hit rehearsals and live shows with renewed enthusiasm – demonstrating this at a later show sharing a bill with Kiffmeyer's new band, The Ne'er Do Wells. As Armstrong recalled, "John was playing really hard, trying to make it look like he was the man, and one thing you cannot do to Tre Cool is outdrum him. One of the first songs we played was 'Longview', which is a great drummer's song, and from that point on, it was like, 'Dude, you're so over'."

After laying down six tracks of new material at Livermore's suggestion (he was a little surprised to learn that this was all they had), Green Day's new and now permanent core line-up refocused and came back to the studio in late 1991 for a new album, Kerplunk!. Although the Lookout label had a more stable financial backing by this stage and Green Day could afford to take more time over their efforts, nonetheless they raced through it and finished it off in four days with a bill of less than $2000.

The die was cast. By this point America had begun to hear of Green Day and the album sold 10,000 copies on its first day on sale – a huge achievement for such a tiny record label. By the end of 1992 it had sold five times that and the band were clearly on the brink of major success. Tours in the UK, Europe, America and Canada established the Green Day brand at grass-roots level and the trio put in their time, building up a following from scratch that is hard to envisage in today's stadium-rock world. Their preferred mode of transport was a mobile library from the Phoenix municipal system, a Bookmobile, which Tre's father fixed up and even drove on occasion.

They left their mark wherever they went: as Livermore

recalled, "I was on tour with the Mr. T Experience in Poland, not long after the Communist government had fallen, and as we pulled into Bialystok, the last town before the Russian border, I thought, 'This has got to be the first time an American punk rock band has played in this part of the world'. Then I saw the huge 'Green Day' spraypainted across the town's water tower. They'd been there, done that, months before us."

On their UK tour of 1991, Green Day even put on a horrible stage show, as Armstrong recalled: "We did a Christmas play. We made the whole crowd sit down on the floor. Tre was the Virgin Mary, Mike was Santa Claus and the narrator and I was the Schizo three wise men."

"And we had our friend Shaun, who has long brown hair just like JC," added Tre. "He came out between my legs and we had ketchup squirting everywhere all over my nice Virgin Mary outfit. We also threw a placenta out into the crowd. We made a placenta with rice pudding and tomato sauce."

Early Green Day shows were hectic, to say the least, with fans screaming out mid-song for a different tune to be played. "They've always done that," said Mike. "That's why we don't have a set list. We play to the reaction of the crowd to some extent. We don't play everything they yell. We have somewhat of a format that we play, but we've never had set lists, at least not after our first tour. The day of our first tour we threw away our set lists and said, let's not use them ever again. So we don't. Decide what songs you're gonna play and have some that you can work around too, for energy-wise. If the crowd's not real energetic we're gonna try to make more energy, and if it's too energetic then we've got to give them a break, slow things down a bit, becuase you don't want anyone getting hurt or anything... some people get pissed off yelling, 'Play this, play this!' Like a guy at one of our shows was like, 'Play 'Knowledge', play 'Knowledge'!' This was out in Rhode Island. And I was mouthing to him, 'We will, we will!' But he couldn't hear me and he was all, 'Man, fuck you!' Totally got irate. And I came over and he's all, 'Man, I give you respect. Man, fuck you!' But I talked to him and I said, 'Hey. Did you hear what I said? I said we will, and you said fuck you to me anyway. You know what, fuck you!' And all of his friends laughed at him. He was like, 'I'm sorry.' 'Yeah, think about what you're doing first. If I hadn't played Knowledge, would you leave the show hating us?' It's one of those things, I mean we can't play every song that everybody wants us to play, but we can try to suffice with the majority of ones that we feel are going to please everyone."

As for the classic punk rock sport of audience participation, Dirnt reasoned: "I don't mind stage diving, just as long as people are courteous of others. If there's five or 10 people standing around and they're not packed together and a guy just jumps on them and lands all of his weight on one guy's neck, that's wrong, or a girl's neck for that matter. I would say 60-40 the girls have taken the bulk of the landings on this tour. It's pretty brutal. Like five-foot tall, 120-pound girls in the front catching these 200-pound dudes jumping out. And this guy who was jumping off the top was like 180 pounds. He jumped off twice and the second time he jumped off he knocked himself out. He was out cold. He was literally passed out. Everybody got out of the way, he hit the ground and they had to drag him outside. It was like, you're an idiot... if something like that happens, we stop.

Actually we stopped when they found him, because the guy was an idiot. I mean, you shouldn't jump from that high. And this crowd was spaced out too. It wasn't like completely packed."

The banbd's own inevitable leap into the big corporate world of music wasn't long in coming, and Green Day pulled the plug on Livermore's management and record label in mid 1993. The break wasn't an easy one for anyone – band, manager, local

fanbase – but the band made it clean and honest. As Livermore recalled, "Back in Berkeley I kept hearing rumours that the major labels were chasing Green Day. The next time I saw Tre, I asked him what was going on. He hummed and hawed, but I'd known him too long for him to be able to keep a secret. 'We're talking to a management firm,' he finally said, and when I rounded up Billie and Mike for a meeting in a nearby café, I found out they were doing more than just talking: they'd already signed a deal."

It emerged that after a bidding war, the band had signed with Warner Brothers subsidiary Reprise, the label set up by Frank Sinatra many years before, after negotations by their new managers, Elliot Cahn and Jeff Saltzman (who also had Mudhoney, Melvins and Primus on their roster). They had also fended off approaches by Epitaph, Geffen and Sony. The bridge between talent and label was Reprise/Warners A&R man Rob Cavallo (the son of Prince/Alanis Morissette manager Bob Cavallo), who said, "I'll never forget when Green Day said to me – it was so cool – they said, 'We're going to be a great band'. And they knew it. 'We're going to be a great band no matter what Reprise does for us.' They could already draw 1000 kids in a good 10 or 12 cities across this country, and they'd already played Europe. These kids were 21 years old. They knew what it took to be successful in the music business. They never had jobs. They made their living by being a band by the time they were age sixteen or seventeen."

Mike later explained of the switch: "The main reason we switched labels, it took us over a year to make the decision, because there comes a point where 15 and 16 year old kids can't put on 600 to 900 people shows. So you end up dealing with medium-size club promoters, and a lot of those guys are really sleazy. If you have no legal stance, then they're just gonna rob you. Three out of four shows on our tour were being cancelled because the fire marshal would show up and close down this punk club – either fully close the club or just close the show down and alert the police and the fire marshal to these clubs. All that's doing is damage to punk shows. And then we're getting all these people going, 'Look at all these other jerks showing up at your shows'. I've had people come up to me now and go, 'Man, look at these people you draw to your shows now, look at them all'. I'd say, 'You know what, man, you're fucking racist'. That's a problem. If I meet someone and they're a jock or I meet someone and they're different than me in any way, if they're a nice person I'll shake their hand, but if they're an asshole and they're letting me know it, I'm gonna tell them they're an asshole. Our music wasn't created strictly for punks. But it was put out and we did play to punks because our friends were punks and we like to hang out and do the punk circuit. And I felt that we gave a lot of the best of us. We've played close to 1000 punk shows now and it really takes its toll out on you. And it really hurts even more when I hear people saying, 'Well now kids at my school are gonna like your music, 'cause it's like the trendy thing to do blah blah blah'. To me that's kind of selfish. Yeah, but you had the music when it first came out there, be glad that you had it years ago. That's how I feel about it. I get people that are mad at us just for that and that alone. We don't want to draw any of those legal aspects into punk shows, into the punk scene at all. We were drawing a lot of people who didn't understand punk shows, so there would be fights going on. It was all leading to one thing, either quit or go on. So we're going on."

After the deal was struck with Reprise – a large label not known for the kind of pop-punk that Green Day were in the process of recording for their breakthrough album, Dookie – Livermore heard an advance tape and he was impressed. "Their first two albums combined had taken less than a week to record;

they spent more time than that just setting up the drum sounds for Dookie. When it was done, they brought me an advance copy, and I was amazed. It was the same Green Day I had always known and loved, only about a hundred times better produced."

The production was key – the album sounded huge. Asked about the controversial differences between being on Reprise and Lookout, Mike explained: "There's a big difference between when you spend a lot of money on a record and when you spend $1500 to $700 on a record. Which is the totals of our other records, $700 for the first record and $1500 for the second record. We had some time to actually pay attention to what we were doing. The reason things are louder is because you're doing things in a more contained environment, you've got a bigger studio, better equipment. The whole album sounds bigger. That's the main difference between any major label album and any independent album, because the independent albums are recorded on a small budget and they sound transistor to some extent... like the real high end... and the low end doesn't kick as much as everything else. That's not a problem... I love that. But radio and TV – a lot of people have a hard time listening to things that aren't incredibly audible. Like my dad would tell me 'God, the quality of your records... the songs are good and everything, but the quality is so lo-fi.' Well, that's what we're recording as, and I think we obtained the same sound that we would have obtained if the other ones had they been on a major label."

Despite his initial qualms ("As good as the record was, though, I wasn't sure their new label would know what to do with it. The kind of music that Green Day played was still very much a cult sound at the end of 1993. Lookout Records specialised in that sound, and we had a built-in audience for it, but Reprise Records, no matter how big they were, didn't") Livermore wished them well, and exits the long, strange story of Green Day at this point. After their enormous success in the

1990s, however, he would often be approached to re-tell the story of their early days in newspapers and magazines.

Back in Berkeley, news had somehow reached MTV and other big-money music organisations that Green Day were hot and their new album was hotter. With media people crawling all over the East Bay, it was clearly time for Green Day to bid the Gilman Street club farewell, not least because of the club's no-major-labels policy. However, a Christmas 1993 show saw them slip through under an assumed name: the crowd, perfectly wise to what was going on, danced and sang with a certain sadness, knowing that part of their own micro-scene was about to depart forever.

It wasn't all wistful sadness, though: there was concrete anger too, directed at the band from some of the Gilman fans for their supposed defection. Green Day – who once revealed that on visiting Gilman Street after the release of Dookie, they were spurned, with one former friend asking "What the hell are you guys doing here?" – were hurt a little by the rejection of the scene that had nurtured them, it seems. Mike Dirnt said: "You know, every band who sold records is getting the sell-out label, especially from fans who liked them in their early, unsuccessful days. They think they've found something, they identify with you because you're underdogs, and then you make it and they hate you. They feel you've betrayed them because now others like you, too. We didn't start the band to cash in a lot of money. When we started out, punk was probably the most unpopular music around."

Billie Joe had loved the Gilman Street days, it appears, saying with evident remorse: "We've played in front of 2000 and 3000 people, and I still haven't felt the same thing that I felt playing that place. There are bad shows I've had there that I'll remember for the rest of my life, and there's the greatest shows I've ever played... Punk is not just the sound, the music:

punk is a lifestyle. There are a lot of bands around that claim to be punk and they only play the music, they have no clue what it's all about. It's a lifestyle I choose for myself. It's not about popularity and all that crap. When we started out we played punk rock, the music, but we developed, we changed our sound but we didn't change. We're just as punk as we used to be. We got a lot of crap, and we're still getting it, for being signed with a major label, so what?"

"There's going to be people who will be bummed out," he told 360 Degrees before the move. "People ask, "Why are you doing this?" and basically, it's because I fucking want to. The music hasn't changed. We're not changing ourselves to suit some big corporate record label. The music will be there if you want to listen to it."

"We wanted to go from an independent to a major," he added to Kerrang!. "We got an offer from Epitaph, but we were like, 'do we want to be on an independent pretending to be a major, or do we want to be on a real major?' We chose to go to Reprise."

Armstrong has always remained completely honest about the home-made punk scene that made him, waxing lyrical on many occasions about the ethos of the late-80s punk scene: "I've even gone as far as saying we're not a punk band any more… but no matter what, that's still gonna stick with me forever, because I love the music, I love the energy of a new band coming out that creates this sense of urgency about 'em. I'll never be able to kick that habit. I love hangin' out with my friends who have small fanzines – kids just writing their guts out about whatever the hell's bothering 'em, and putting it on a Xerox machine and then handing it out for a quarter apiece at shows or at a party. All I wanna do is just try and work it out. I was sitting there the other day, counting all the records that the Replacements put out, stuff like that, and thinking how [Paul] Westerberg totally came across to his audience and did everything, everything that he wanted to do in music. He wasn't extremely successful for it, but the guy has influenced people, and a lot of 'em don't even know that they are influenced by him."

But all this angst would prove to be both short-lived and irrelevant. When Dookie was released on 5 November 1994, the world and his dog went Green Day crazy. The band had staked more or less everything they had on the accompanying tour breaking the album for them – after all, many a rock act had made the jump from indie to major label and fallen flat when their new paymasters weren't rewarded with major sales. As Billie said, "I was sleeping on someone else's mattress. It was someone else's room. I put my clothes in a garbage bag, grabbed my guitar and my four-track, and I left."

MTV helped assist Dookie's progress with their constant rotation of the 'Longview' single, and the iconic, chaotic sleeve of the album helped etch its presence into the public consciousness still further. The album took its title from a slang word for excrement: "Dookie is slang for shit," Billie giggled. "It was going to be called Liquid Dookie, but we thought that was too gross!"

In 1994, the impact that the album made on the music world was far greater than it would be today. Consider the following. In April that year, just seven months before Dookie appeared, Nirvana's Kurt Cobain ended the reign of grunge – with all the joyless introspection and sadness that went with it – his own band and his own life with a single shotgun cartridge. In the wake of his death, alternative music fans wondered in shock what would come next. Grunge had wiped out most of the tinny, laughable glam-metal, funk-metal and thrash metal movements at a stroke, leaving only the biggest of the pack (Metallica and the Red Hot Chili Peppers are notable examples) surviving in its wake. It was clearly time for a change of focus – and Green Day, with their insane antics, enormous irreverence and stupidity-for-stupidity's-sake lifestyle seemed to fulfil the necessary criteria. One journalist pointed out at the time that Kurt Cobain sometimes wore a dress on stage as a metaphor for the women's struggle against objectification, but Billie Joe Armstrong did the same because that way it was easier to moon the drummer. Wise words.

Shortly after the move to Reprise, Mike carried out a revealing fanzine interview in which he discussed the agonies of touring with no money. Recalling his recent youth (he was still only 21 at the time), he laughed: "We went to school in the suburbs. It was really shitty. One year the high school I went to was really shitty. But then I went to a school that was somewhat more alternative. But there were still a lot of shitheads and everything. There were alternative kids, but you still got fucked with a lot. Kinda lame... Just sitting around a lousy town. We come from a town where everyone looks forward to their senior ball and their boyfriends and girlfriends."

On the subject of drugs, he pondered: "In the Bay Area a lot of people do a lot of speed and a lot of drugs. And they just sit around and they'd rather work shitty nine-to-five jobs and waste out, instead of actually getting out there and doing what they would rather be doing. Their only limitation is that they're in this suburban subculture. The thing with subcultures is... it's just too much of a bad thing."

Asked about the 'Longview' single – which featured some semi-offensive lyrics – he replied: "[Reprise] wanted it and we wanted it. We were actually the ones who were a little more hesitant... [to] see whether or not it would hurt our radio play or anything. But [Reprise] was encouraging it and I thought that was really cool. So we went with it."

Mike was also asked how a forthcoming Green Day show could be as cheap as $5 per ticket, to which he explained: "We lost a lot of money. We basically paid for it out of our own pocket... it's worth it. But there are times when I get really frustrated because kids are yelling at us anyway, thinking we're making a lot of money because we're on a fucking major label. MTV doesn't pay you. Unless kids go out there and buy your records, you're not making anything. We're still not making anything. We've lost thousands of dollars on this tour. Something like $15,000. Doesn't sound like a lot, whatever, but I guess it is. I don't really care about the money thing. I just don't like people rubbing it in my face, saying that I'm a rock star. A rock star is two things, a rock star is an asshole and a rock star is rich. I'm neither of the two. I'm nowhere near either of the two. It really bothers me too. Some people will come up to us and ask us the weirdest questions. Just ask us money questions about this and that. When we're selling our T-shirts for really cheap and we're not making a dime off of them. To keep our T-shirts this low, our merchandise guy gets really upset when people bitch about a $10 T-shirt. Any lower than that and we've got to pay. After this tour, our prices have to go up a little bit, because we can't afford to keep paying to play. This tour has been physically exhausting, playing 10 days on, one day off and that whole day off is driving. Then another six days on, one day off driving. Another 10 days on... this whole tour we've had one day off where we didn't have to drive. So it's physically exhausting. That's how we did it, and it worked out real good... all of the shows have sold out. People have gotten our shirts and that's rad. I don't know if we stepped on our own foot by having people expect $5 shows every time we come around because we can't do it. It's too expensive."

Billie Joe echoed Mike's anti-rock star stance much later on, adding: "A lot of people look at rock stars and movie stars and see people with fast cars and Armani suits and millions of dollars, and look at it as rebellion. That's not rebellion, that's decadence. That's disgusting. That's the reason why I play punk rock to begin with. Just because Joe-Schmo Scumbag is cruising around in a pair of high-heeled shoes and driving a Masarati doesn't mean he's actually walking the walk. So I feel like I have to be focused on what's true and meaningful to me. I'm still wearing the pants I had in the eleventh grade. I hate celebrities. I really hate them... I like people and I'm not a person that just stays in my house all the time and counts my money or anything like that, but I'm not going to go out and try to act like a star. I've got my set of friends – I love them, I think they're great people. I love my wife – she's the best thing that's ever happened to me in the whole world and that is all I need. When I talk about my friends, I'm talking about Mike and Tre."

Of the new wave of grunge, and the pop-punk phenomenon of which they were so much a part, Armstrong reasoned: "The thing is that punk has always been here, it's just that MTV has monopolised the whole thing, inspiring the mainstream to look a little more punk than usual. Like how Mötley Crüe kicked out Vince Neil because they wanted a singer who was more punk. And Lars Ulrich of Metallica shaved his head and grew a goatee... It just seems like everyone was hoping to find the next Nirvana. I want to be completely separate from the whole grunge thing. I don't even think the whole so-called grunge people are even into being called grunge. We played in Florida and this guy with a TV camera, who was totally dressed up in a suit and was from the Fox Network was asking us, 'So what is grunge and what does it mean to you?' We were like, 'This sucks'."

1995 was packed with tours for Green Day, who managed their ascent to fame with relative success. Billie Joe got married and maintained his fidelity despite the world's groupies at his feet, as he told Q magazine in 2005; appearances on talk shows such as The Late Show With David Letterman, The Tonight Show With Jay Leno and Late Night With Conan O'Brian seemed to fall naturally to them; and on magazine covers such as Rolling Stone and Spin they seemed to be entirely at home. The single 'Basket Case', with its video of the band as mental home inmates playing the song while fellow residents shuffle by and nursing staff administer medication, was a classic, and stamped the Green Day mark on popular music with solid intent. Interestingly, the song made no impact on first release in the slightly harder-to-impress UK, although on reissue it became a major hit.

Of the 'pop-punk' tag that had been applied to their music, Armstrong mused: "When we signed to a major, a lot of people said we were using punk rock as a stepping-stone for fame and fortune. People called it 'Gap punk,' but I felt like we were probably an introduction to a kid that's going to buy Black Flag records later on. That's a positive thing. There's a lot of kids now that are really active in the punk rock community, and it has to do with the fact that they got into us first."

"People are still arguing about that stuff," he added. "When we started playing punk rock, it was a proven fact that punk could not get popular. You couldn't become a millionaire off the back of this music. In fact, six or seven years ago, people were afraid to say the 'P' word! We never played punk rock to become famous, and I never thought being obnoxious would make me successful. What I always say to people is, "you can take us out of our punk rock environment, but you can't take the punk rock out of us... When we started out as a band, we played punk rock music, then we changed our sound – but we didn't change who we were. I just like writing songs, and if someone thinks that's some kind of punk rock dichotomy, then they can go fuck themselves."

Only a couple of hindrances prevented the post-Dookie tour from being completely trouble-free: Dirnt's heart condition allegedly led to panic attacks and cancelled dates on a few

occasions, and some European gigs were postponed in '95 as the whole band cited complete exhaustion. But highlights were plentiful: Green Day's legendary set at the slightly cynical Woodstock 2 festival in 1994 (at which the peace and love vibes seemed slightly incongruous in comparison with the constant rain, inadequate facilities and headliners Metallica's $2 million fee) ended in chaos. When festival-goers threw mud at the stage, Billie and Mike asked them to throw more: a torrent of mud followed and the set resembled a mud bath in no time. Then the stage was invaded and a ruckus between crowd members and security officers ensused: the fracas took on a less amusing timbre when Dirnt had teeth knocked out by one of the latter after he was mistaken for a member of the stage-invading audience.

Otherwise, Tre in particular endeared himself to the British music press, walking up to a journalist from a music weekly and placing a cock ring in his hand. That's right, a cock ring – and one that had been in place all day. "Man, he was pissed off!" he told Record Collector. "He got a fistful of my nuts! I had this sweaty ball-ring on my dick and I just handed it to him and said, 'Here, I've been wearing that for hours'. He said, 'Euurgh, you fucker' and ran off to wash his hands. He was a wanker, that's why I did it to him!"

At one show Billie Joe was arrested for exposing his buttocks in public, a ridiculous episode that passed quickly into Green Day folklore. As he recalled, "I dropped the pick and... just mooned the crowd, which is pretty harmless compared to what I've done before. And I wasn't even thinking about it, I just went out and started playing again. Then I went backstage and was hanging out with [my wife] Adrienne, and this guy Jimmy who does security for us goes 'Come on – there's a car waiting for you outside right now. You've gotta get out of here!' I said 'What's wrong?' and he said he didn't even know. So we get in the car and all of a sudden about 10 cops come walking over, fully surrounding the car. So the guy puts the cuffs on me, throws me in the car, and I get tossed in the holding tank for two, three hours. I wasn't in the bullpen. I was in with the other ones, the not-so-bad ones. They made me take all my jewellery out. And my shoe [laces], so I wouldn't hang myself or something."

In 1996 the next album, Insomniac, was released. Critically acclaimed but nowhere near as commercially successful as Dookie, it remains a strange low point in Green Day's career. At the time those who didn't appreciate the band's particular strain of humour labelled it the downfall of the band, but this was far from the case – even if the songs on Insomniac (see track-by-track analysis) weren't as immediately gripping as, say, 'Longview' or 'Basket Case', the band still had their explosive live show to rely on and had no trouble in filling huge venues with crowds.

Of Insomniac, Billie mused: "We have a lot of punk rock in our background, but now, we're just doing something a little bit different. We don't want to stick ourselves in one genre for the rest of our lives. Our live shows have seen a whole new generation of people coming out and I don't have a problem with that at all. You always get nostalgic about certain things from the old days, but we're comfortable doing what we're doing right now. I mean, we had five weeks to make our last record, instead of two days."

"Rock has become so stagnant," he added, "and there are a lot of bands that aren't doing anything different than following the trend. I think the reason hip-hop has become so much bigger than rock lately is because those artists are much more ambitious. They're making records that have a concept and characters. They sound like a script."

Insomniac was a heavier, more aggressive album than Dookie: producer Rob Cavallo said "It's a lot harder, a lot faster, and a lot angrier," and he was right. Part of the album's strength came from its social commentary, for example on 'Geek Stink Breath', a song that addressed the horrors of speed abuse. "It's an ugly song for an ugly drug," said Dirnt. "We have a lot of friends hooked on speed. They're so tweaked out, man, it's ridiculous." Armstrong: "It's not really for it, and it's not really against it. It just describes a state of mind, and the destructiveness it had on me personally. I liked speed because I wanted some rocket fuel. I wanted to think. That's the difference between us and the grunge scene: we wanted to go faster."

Dirnt expanded: "Northern California is kind of one of the methamphetamine capitals of the world. Let's just say we have a lot of friends who've gone that direction. I've dabbled here and there. We all have, but we are not speed freaks. We are insomniacs, but we're not speed freaks. There's a generational thing with a lot of the lyrics on this album. Like 'Geek Stink Breath,' a lot of people 20 or 30 years ago, people don't know what speed is. And they don't know that people who do speed lose their teeth constantly and pick scabs off their face constantly, and it eats holes in their brains, and whatever. But that's really a prevalent thing, where we come from."

Another track, 'Armatage Shanks', was a song about miserable choices, despite its semi-humorous title. Billie Joe: "When I wrote that song, it was right before Dookie came out, and I was really at odds with myself. I was like, man, do I really want to do this? A lot of the time I was thinking about suicide, how it's so easy to kill yourself, but so hard to stay alive. I was in a break-up with my then-girlfriend, a total, raving punk rocker who didn't approve of me being on a major label. She moved down to Ecuador, saying she couldn't live in a world with McDonald's and such. It was fucking me up pretty bad."

Billie knew why Insomniac hadn't sold well, blaming it on lack of promotion in an interview with Rip magazine: "Well, it's like, we didn't set up this record. We didn't. We didn't do any promotion beforehand, we completely quit doing interviews, and basically we just wanted to go on into it. We weren't even sure if we wanted to do a video. And then when we did a video, it got yanked from daytime rotation because people were getting grossed-out by it. So I think we did alienate a lot of people. So that was expected, that it wasn't going to sell a lot of records."

Just after this stage, Green Day fired their managers Elliot Cahn and Jeff Saltzman and became self-managed. Having written a song called 'J.A.R.' (after a friend of Billie Joe's called Jason Andrew Relva who had died in a car crash) for the Angus film soundtrack, Green Day allegedly accused the managers of leaking the song to a radio station for their own promotional purposes. Although it was concluded that no such leak had taken place, band and management parted ways in any case. "The only three people who know what's best for Green Day are me, Billie, and Tre," said Dirnt. "We know sometimes that all we really have is each other," added Armstrong. "This is the three of us, and this is what you get."

Billie Joe wasn't a happy man at this point, it seems – perhaps simply because he was burned out from touring, perhaps for some other reason. Either way, when he talked about himself he could be seriously negative. "Maybe I'm just getting jaded or something," he said. "But I just got cable again and I can't stand anything. Six years ago you could hear something that was different and know that it was different. So it'd be 'alternative' or whatever… I hate all this music that's coming out now – the past year was just hell for music. But people are buying it, so then I'm thinking, maybe they're the ones that are good and I'm the one who sucks?"

More seriously for Green Day, he added: "I just don't know if I really wanna be involved in the rock world any more at all. Period. I don't necessarily have anything against a big record company or people who want to join up with a big record company. It really is right for some people, but more and more, I don't think that I'm really meant to. And I hate to sound like that, because I don't like taking things for granted. I don't like to talk about my problems when there's some kid struggling in his garage somewhere saying 'Fuck him! He's just taking it for granted. Shit, I wish I could do something like that, but I'm just stuck here in Biloxi, Mississippi, and I can't even get a gig'. I'm so confused right now."

Perhaps some of this came from the perception that punk – the music he loved and which had shaped him – was becoming a corporate commodity like any other brand. "We became what we hated," he snarled. "Which is, the people I despised in high school – and now – are buying our records. We initially became a trend, so there was no way I expected to sell as many records with Insomniac as with Dookie. That's one of the biggest-selling

records of the decade. We get slagged by the punk rockers, and it's like, I don't blame them. If you draw that much attention to yourself, that's what you're gonna get – attention – and it's not personal any more… There isn't a day goes by in the past year and a half that I haven't thought about quitting. I went to this party on New Year's Eve, and this band Juke, and another band, the Tantrums, played in a friend of mine's backyard. And a lot of my old friends showed up, and everybody was just dancing. And I was dancing, and getting really muddy, and I was having a great time. I can't remember the last time I sat down and listened to a record from beginning to end and felt this incredible spine-chilling music. And it's because I haven't been able to go out and watch bands play at my free will. I'm not gonna live in a closet, I'm not gonna vegetate myself."

Frazzled by touring, Armstrong snapped, "I get so irritated by people. I think I'm more bitter than I've ever been in my whole life, to tell you the honest truth. I think Insomniac is much more of a bitter record than Dookie. And I think the older people get, the more they kinda get angry. I think a lot of people feel like they get cheated by life somehow – no-one is ever completely satisfied. There's maybe a few. But I mean, I'm in a place where I don't really wanna be. It's like, sometimes I feel like we're losing our passion for playing music. And that's the fucked-up thing, when you lose passion for what you love, then it's like, is this marriage headed for divorce or what?"

He added: "I'm just not enjoying life right now. I'm really not. I'm so cluttered, I can't even speak. Yeah, I do feel like I'm getting old, and I'm kinda bitter about that. I'm not excited about being onstage any more, and I was really trying to convince myself that I was. Really. Before we did this last US tour, every time I did an interview… I was like 'Yeah! I'm excited! I wanna play these arenas!' and stuff. And then just every night, it started sucking, it felt like a routine or something. It felt almost choreographed in a lot of ways. And I was yelling 'fuck you!' to people, but I didn't know who I was yelling 'fuck you' to any more… I think it's just the stress of getting up in front of all those people all the time, every day. It's like, "Do I really feel like downing another fucking pot of coffee and a bottle of wine before I walk onstage to do this again? Just to get myself ready to go?' You know, for all those people. And every night I always do something different and stupid. But at the same time, it'd be really cool to just say 'Fuck you!' to people and like, walk off. And then they'd get it. It's like, 'I'm really telling you to fuck off this time! Time to pack up and go home'. It'd just be so nice to start from scratch again."

During the layoff after the tour, Billie Joe is said to have written over 50 songs in preperation for Green Day's next album, Nimrod. With everything to prove – not least the naysayers' affirmation that Green Day's career was effectively over after Dookie – the band promoted Nimrod with endless energy. The album, which featured guest appearances on two songs by members of the ska-pop-punk band No Doubt, showcased a slightly darker, more aggressive band, which was reflected in their activities: after a secret warm-up gig at Johnny Depp's Viper Room club in LA, the band were criticised for trashing a Tower Records branch that was hosting a signing session (Billie scrawled 'Fuck you' and 'Nimrod' on the windows in black spray-paint). A later session at radio station KROQ's annual acoustic Christmas show, Green Day threw the stage Christmas tree into the crowd and wrote obscenities on the stage. Police were called but no arrests were made. More shenanigans included a visit to Japan to play at the Mount Fuji Rock Festival: when the appearance was cancelled due to a typhoon, the band spent time at an amusement park instead, riding on the attractions with Beck, Prodigy, the Foo Fighters, and the Red Hot Chili Peppers. Reportedly, Tre – accidentally or otherwise – shot a member of the Foo Fighters with an airgun, requiring Billie Joe to step in and defuse the injured party's anger.

Yet again Tre Cool was making firm friends with other bands on the road. As he recalled, "We were staying at the Chateau Marmont Hotel for six months recording a record, and the drummer from that English, old, stuffy band called Radiohead moves in next door for a few days. We're partying in my room, having a good time with the stereo on, drinking, whatever. Then I see this guy walking out of my room with a bathrobe on. I'm like, 'what the fuck is this? Who's in my fucking room?' and my friends are like, 'Oh, that was the guy next door, he said to turn it down'. I'm like, 'Oh, really?' It was on at that point... I got some rope and I put a slipknot around his doorknob. Then I went over across the way to a handrail and then tied it securely to the handle. In the morning, when he was trying to get to his gig at Coachella, he couldn't open the door and he had to call security to come let him out. He started shouting, 'You let me out! I'm telling Thom!' I'm like, 'Dude, if you walk into a room of hot chicks, you're like, 'Word up!' Right?"

Add to this the litany of soundbites which Tre has amassed over the years and you have a living punk legend. Witness the wisdom of Tre on sex ("Sometimes you jack off so much that you get blackheads all over your dick. You get athlete's cock"); on booze ("The night before last we were drinking as much as we could so that we could piss out of our window in Madrid. Taxi drivers were putting their hands out and going, 'is it raining?'"); and on constipation ("What you should do is get some cereal in the morning before you go and cover it in crystal meth. You get as high as heels and the cereal will pass through before you leave the house. It's got the fibre to push through anything that is stuck in the colon. I'm an asshole expert!").

Although stories such as these paint Green Day in true rock'n'roll colours, Dirnt is quick to point out the other side of

43

the band: "I don't think we have the typical touring musician lifestyle. Well, we work a hard shift – we hit the road every night – but we don't stay in hotels. We have the most exciting job on tour, because we get to play every day and we live for that, but we also have the most boring job on tour, you know, doing interviews and standing around all day hurrying up and waiting. So it's a hard one for sure. But playing music is so much fun. I love my job!"

"I just try not to put myself on a pedestal and think it's more than it is," he added. "You have to remember you're here today and gone later today. We don't go out and buy Ferraris and throw the rock'n'roll lifestyle. We've been weaned into it really well. We'd been going on tour for years before we ever got to a major label. We'll go on tour for months, and then when we come back, our friends will give us a head check. That's been happening for years. We'll leave for two months, come back, leave for three months, come back, and every time, our friends give us a head check. I think that we're pretty firmly grounded in who we are and where we come from."

"With Nimrod I think... we consciously did try to change a bit," pondered Billie, "[thinking that] if we couldn't take the challenge, we'd end up like some old punk rockers, playing the same stuff over and over – that's a fate worse than death... I don't want to limit myself musically. All I want to do is write good songs. I want to develop and go into different styles, cross my boundaries of the two-and-a-half minute punk song with a three-and-a-half minute jazz song. Maybe get into a little bit of swing or rockabilly... Whatever we do in the past, we leave that and go to the next chapter. We always want to try to keep reinventing ourselves and come out with something new. We're just trying to make something that documents where we're at in this particular time. We always want to make the best record we possibly can."

While Nimrod benefited from the endless controversy caused by its creators, it too failed to approach the phenomenal sales total of Dookie, and there was a palpable sense that perhaps the band were on a gentle career slide. Certainly the fact that they spent almost the whole of 1998 and 1999 on tour rather than creating anything new to convince people otherwise didn't help, although a prestigious headlining slot on the Vans Warped Tour with then-popular punk and punk-related acts such as the Mighty Mighty Bosstones, Jurassic 5, Long Beach Dub Allstars, The Donnas, MXPX, and NOFX in 2000 kept their profile high. Of the long period of apparent inactivity, Dirnt countered: "We took a break from the public eye, but we worked our asses off. Once again, we enjoy what we do. It's really fun. We set ourselves up in a studio environment. It really was a 100 percent creative environment. The only rule was, 'If you've got nothing, record something'. Everything we did inspired the next move for this album… It's a matter of making sure you don't get bored and always keep creative. Whether it is Tre going in the studio and doing a polka song, or me going in and doing an acoustic thing, or Billie doing something else, it's being creative and not pigeonholing yourself. We kind of feel the art of the album can get lost in the routine for a lot of musicians: you make a record, put out a single, make a video, go on tour – this kind of mundane routine. We just like to keep things interesting for ourselves, and dangerous. Rock and roll should be dangerous."

However, on first spin many fans were dismayed by Warning, released in October 2000 after the Vans tour came to a halt. Although the usual Green Day staple elements – melodic choruses, layered riffs and pounding percussion – were all present and correct, there was a sense that the band had strayed too far into experimental territory. One of the songs,'Time Of Your Life (Good Riddance)', was nothing less than an acoustic ballad with orchestral and bagpipes (!) accompaniment, and – like the Chili Peppers' 'Under The Bridge' and Metallica's 'Nothing Else Matters' – was hated by the old-school fanbase. Why? Simply because the very palatable, easy to digest, radio-friendly tune was snapped up by mainstream media and presented to the non-punk-buying public as a side of Green Day that people could consume without ever having heard a single punk song, by Green Day or anybody else. Such was the song's impact that it was selected to soundtrack the last ever episode of cult US comedy Seinfeld, thus introducing Green Day to millions of Americans who might otherwise have never shown any interest in them.

Of 'Good Riddance (Time of Your Life)', Billie said: "Putting that song on the record made me nervous," he says. "For me to kind of step out and challenge myself and our crowd – to say there is beauty in life, there is hope – well, that song has freed us in a lot of respects." And of the album, he added: "We wanted to bring in new instruments," says Armstrong of the decision, "but we didn't want to lose the energy that me, Mike, and Tre have when we're in a room together, but it's fun to bring in harmonicas and mandolins and, you know, a mariachi band or whatever."

"The thing that people should realise," he added, "is that I've always listened to all kinds of great songwriters, from Bikini Kill, to The Rolling Stones, to The Replacements... just good songs. I'm definitely more influenced by songwriters than punk... I think before we're a punk band, before I'm a punk rocker, I'm a songwriter."

Asked by one interviewer if he had become more of a songwriter with Warning, Armstrong reasoned, "I don't want to live in an ivory tower, being the songwriter who just turns inward. I always want to be a part of the whole thing. That's why I live a pretty normal life at home, go shopping, all that.

It's part of my life and I don't want to have that part of my life taken from me... You can never tell if your fans will like an album or if they won't, and I'm not gonna sit and try to market myself to anybody. If you feel like getting into this record, then do it. If you don't, then don't. It's as simple as that. I know a lot of people are going to call me arrogant and all that, but I don't care. If somebody likes our songs, they should like them for the right reason and not just for marketing."

Not for the first time, he added that his punk background wouldn't limit his musical ambitions: "I don't want to paint myself into a corner; punk will always be a part of my life. But I don't want to limit myself musically. On Warning we managed to test how far we can go. I love punk and punk songs will always be part of Green Day. But it would be really limiting if we'd neglect something we really want to do, like explore other styles of music...A lot of people just saw us as some three-riff punk band who couldn't really play. I don't mind what they say about us. I know that we always tried out new things. One thing they can't pin on us is that we never experimented or that we recorded the same album over and over again."

Of the record's most scathing moment, 'Fashion Victim', he pondered: "I think what is going on in America is extreme, more than extreme. The youth cult, they worship youth so much it's almost paranoid. And LA is the Mecca of it all; it's where they're taking it to the hilt. People are so damned afraid that one day they might wake up and discover that they've grown old. I don't like LA. I'm sure there are some great people there but the majority just seem to be so artificial. Look at how they worship everything they think is fashionable. Isn't it sick? Nothing is stupid enough as long as it's fashion and a sign of youth. If Britney would paint her ass green, I'm sure you could spot green asses all over LA as soon as the word was out."

After this point, Green Day seemed to put creativity on hold, instead choosing to release not one but two career compilations. The first was a greatest hits album called (with sardonic glee) International Superhits, boosted by two new tracks, 'Maria' and 'Poprocks And Coke'. This was accompanied by a DVD, as had become de rigueur in the new multimedia era. It didn't take long to pass the gold mark, and was swiftly followed up by Shenanigans, a B-sides and rarities collection that seemed aimed directly at the older fanbase.

In 2002 Green Day toured on the Pop Disaster package with Blink-182 and Jimmy Eat World. The collaboration was interesting: by this stage in their careers, Green Day had witnessed the rise of more than a few pop-punk acts influenced directly by them rather than the older, 1980s bands that had shaped Green Day themselves. Of these, Blink-182 were the obvious forerunners, combining numbnuts slapstick foolery with ultra-catchy pop tunes with the occasional punk riff. Sum 41 were another, less successful act with obvious Green Day influences; ironically, Blink would be placed higher on the bill on more than a few festivals in the early years of the Noughties.

"We met Sum 41 and the Blink guys," said Tre of the new contenders. "They're good guys. They sell a lot of records, but they're more like boy bands. They're really polished; they're an easier pill to swallow for a lot of kids. But at least it gets kids into music that has guitars in it. It's a lot better to have some stuff to lure them over to the dark side, right?"

No-one was fooling Green Day, despite the rise of the pop-punk army. As Billie Joe said, "I think the whole 'rebirth' of punk rock is a load of shit. Six or seven years ago, people were afraid to say the 'P' word, and now everyone claims to have seen the Jam back in '77, when they probably opened up for Pink Floyd and everybody hated them… I chose this lifestyle. When we started playing punk rock, it was a proven fact that punk could not get popular. So we never played punk rock to become

49

famous. People now use the phrase 'post-punk' like it's after the fact which is the worst label I've ever heard. Sometimes I think because we're this big band now, because we've made a lot of money, we've become totally redundant – we're not punk rock any more. But then I think about it and just say, 'you can take us out of our punk rock environment, but you can't take the punk rock out of us', you know what I mean?"

"Those people missed the 80s, when punk rock was underground," added Tre. "That was when great bands like Nomeansno, Minor Threat and the Dead Kennedys were travelling around the world in vans. Punk was a four-letter word for a long time."

Apart from a soundtrack appearance for the film New Guy with the song 'Outsider' and an arrest for Armstrong (he was pulled over for speeding, failed a sobriety test and was released from jail the following morning), 2003 was a quiet year for Green Day, who spent much time writing and recording a new album. By this stage a little critical respect was being afforded to them as a so-called 'classic' band with over a decade under their collective belts – VH-1's 100 Best Songs Of The Past 25 Years feature included 'Time Of Your Life (Good Riddance)' at number 78 and Rolling Stone placed Dookie at number 193 in their 500 Greatest Albums of All Time. Although many observers assumed that Green Day would never regain the critical praise they had gained in earlier days, it was clear that a degree of affection – perhaps a patronising affection, but still affection nonetheless – lingered for them among the writers and editors who had grown from frat-boy punk lovers to respectable family men since the high times of 'Basket Case'.

All this was completely blown away by the release of the 'American Idiot' single in late 2004 and then the parent album of the same name. Both topped the US and Canadian charts, becoming their first US number 1 album in the process, and sold vast amounts worldwide (the album sold over 267,000 copies in its first week of release). The commercial impact of the album was so huge that all previous debate over the relative values of the Green Day career trajectory seemed irrelevant, with American Idiot easily the most important album of their career (with the possible exception of Dookie, which had broken them in the first place). The follow-up single, the mellow but dark 'Boulevard Of Broken Dreams', stayed at the top of the Billboard Modern Rock Tracks chart for 16 weeks, and a massive world tour backed up the campaign. By early 2005 American Idiot was double platinum and rising and scooped Green Day a fistful of Grammy nominations – Best Rock Album, Album of the Year, Record of the Year, Best Rock Song, Best Rock Vocal Performance By A Duo Or Group, and Best Music Video (Short Form), all for the album or leadoff single. The band played at the ceremony, appeared on the cover of Rolling Stone, and saw a reissue of 'Time Of Your Life (Good Riddance)' go platinum.

But hold on, it didn't end there. Music fans watched in near-catatonic shock as the awards, live achievements, chart hits and sales certifications rolled in, including Kid's Choice Award for Favorite Music Group, a performance on Saturday Night Live, singles chart dominance with 'Holiday' and 'Wake Me Up When September Ends', the video for 'Boulevard Of Broken Dreams' taking no fewer than six MTV Video Music Awards (Video of the Year, Best Group Video, Best Rock Video, Best Direction [Samuel Bayer], Best Cinematography [Samuel Bayer], and Best Editing [Tim Royes]), the video for 'American Idiot' winning Viewer's Choice and a nomination for Best Art Direction. By the time of writing, American Idiot is quadruple platinum and counting. Got all that?

If not, add these to the pile: Green Day then played as part of ReAct Now: Music & Relief in aid of victims of Hurricane Katrina and scooped two American Music Awards for Favorite Pop/Rock Album and Favorite Alternative Artist, were nominated for Favorite Pop/Rock Band/Duo/Group and Artist of the Year and a Grammy Award for Record of the Year ('Boulevard Of Broken Dreams'). Billie Joe rounded off the year by appearing on the cover of Rolling Stone once again.

The big question is: why? And how? And, well, why again? The story of American Idiot and how it blew Green Day right up into the stratosphere merits an entire book of its own, but in brief – which is all we have space for here – there are several identifiable reasons why the album became so huge.

First and most obviously, American Idiot attacks the America of George W. Bush with unprecedented venom. Disgusted by the Iraq war, which had been burbling along since March 2003 – the early days of post-9/11 paranoia – and claiming the lives of many American and British servicemen and untold thousands of Iraqi citizens, Armstrong laid out all his feelings on the table. In doing so he ignited a spark that had been dormant in American youth – and, importantly, some fairly middle-aged music fans

– that gave the album a relevance and a power that was not felt elsewhere.

"What this album screams is that my band and I aren't represented by this government run by George Bush and his cronies," said Dirnt. "They don't represent my moral stance. They don't hold my values, and if you ignore the way things are going today, no matter what you do, you're living in a fantasy… We were compelled to make this album. This album says that you're losing your individuality. You're pissed off. You're being misrepresented. It says that I don't know what I want, but I do know that I don't want to be an American idiot… Any sales or acclaim or anything is nice, but this album is about making a statement. We want people to buy it but also understand where we're coming from. That's so important."

"I wish we had a President who didn't lie to us every day. President Bush happened to us and everyone living America," he added. "We didn't elect this President. We elected somebody else. An old standing rule got him in. The electoral college got him in and that was set up a long time ago so the people who had an education made sure they elected the President, as opposed to the populace. It worked, but it doesn't seem like those people are very educated."

Of American Idiot's inspiration, Armstrong remembered: "Reality television meets news and war. Tanks going into Baghdad with splashes of Viagra commercials in between. I was so confused about what was going on, I had to write about it. All my songwriting is about creating a statement and taking action. As time has gone on, and because of the climate around me, I've just felt more responsibility to think about politics. I've always written about what's around me, whether it's about being a kid masturbating in front of the television, or now, being scared to death in front of the television." As for Bush himself? "I think he's one of the worst presidents the US has ever had," he said, simply. "I'll just keep writing songs, and hopefully, one day he'll get tried for war crimes."

No other cultural message was as hard or as stylish, which leads me to the second point – American Idiot is a damn fine album in its own right. Styled around the ambitious but gripping concept dreamed up by Billie Joe of a flawed character called St. Jimmy, whose fool's progress is followed through the suite of connected tunes, the record is at once digestible in bites and a whole, interrelated thematic experience. Finally, it looked good – and so did the band. Decked out in the uniform of the times – a semi-Gothic, semi-androgynous mix of eye makeup and black suits, the band, the videos and the very album sleeve looked, well, gorgeous. Not bad for three sweaty punks from the East Bay…

Perhaps the biggest question raised by the success of American Idiot is, how punk can a stadium band be, when millions of dollars are invested in its every move and it has attained the status of a corporation? This issue – the identity of punk, and how it relates to material success – has cropped up time and again in our story, and is no nearer being solved at its end that at its beginning. Billie Joe once talked at length about it, saying: "I just don't know how to fit into rock music any more. I don't know what I like about it any more. I don't like anything about it any more, to tell you the truth… the whole thing with the mainstreaming of punk rock. I just feel lost in the whole thing... The thing is, a lot of musicians have gotten so comfortable with this big so-called 'revolution in rock music' over the past decade. First it was like, 'Fuck the corporations! Fuck the corporations!" And then people just sorta got cosy with that, and forgot that these bands are getting lost in the shuffle. And I'm talking about the ones that never get noticed at all and just get kinda bitter. The 15 minutes of fame is getting shorter and shorter. And now music is totally going backwards

– the first half of [the 1990s], there were a few things going on that were interesting. It wasn't my favorite kind of music, but it had a sensibility about it. If you think about Nirvana and Pearl Jam and that whole Seattle scene, and even the Offspring – there was this thing going on that was more honest, in a lot of ways. It wasn't like, beer, drugs and pussy, like what went on through the 80s with all the hair bands. But now what we've got is Hootie & the Blowfish... they are nice regular guys. And they're totally comfortable with that, and they sort of put that out, to where they don't really have... I dunno, there's a certain amount of attitude that, say, someone like Cobain or Vedder has that they don't have. But it's becoming way not... real any more or something. Maybe not real to me. It's just turning back into what it was in the 80s. It's like, 'Hey, everyone! We're Huey Lewis & The News!'"

Money is, in punk as in everywhere else, the root of all evil to Green Day – or at least to their fans, as Dirnt recalled. "One question we get asked a lot now is 'How much money do you make?' When I was younger, I actually asked that question to my mom's friend. My mom took me and slapped me in the face and said, 'Do not ask that question! It's none of your business'. Sure, we make money. We make plenty of money. And it's peace of mind for me to know that I've bought my mom a house, and that my little sisters don't have to live in a trailer any more."

Armstrong added: "The fucked-up thing about being famous and having money is that if you complain about something, people are like, 'What the fuck are you complaining about? You don't have to work a real job. You don't have to worry about money, or a place to live'. I feel like I don't have anyone to vent my frustrations to because they won't understand."

This attitude was, he hinted, a throwback to his own youth: "I fucking hate college students, to tell you the truth, because they've been able to go to school, get an education, live in the dorms, and get a free ride from their parents. I'm also envious, because I never had that opportunity to learn. I wrote a song... called 'Brat' about waiting for your parents to die so you can get your inheritance. Which my son will probably be singing one day himself."

Make no mistake: Green Day knew that they were asking a lot from their fans when they released American Idiot. After all, it was a concept album about a war that might or might have found sympathy among the masses, from a band whose career had been sliding gently downward for years. "It was scary," admitted Mike. "For lack of a better analogy, I've been saying it's like we got this mountain we already climbed, only this time we took a different route. And on the way there we saw one higher. Which one do you want to climb? The view at the top of the other mountain doesn't suck, but you always want to challenge yourself. And if we are doing that and stirring up controversy, it always seems like we get into good things that way."

As for the concept idea, he laughed: "We drew a lot of inspiration from a band like Outkast or Eminem and those guys who are so ambitious with rap. They don't let their ambitions stop them in the studio. Granted, they don't pull the stuff off live. To try to pull it off live is a little bit scary. I do feel there are a lot of younger bands today whose Beatles and Stones collections are getting further and further back in their collection and they need to pull them to the front again... Whenever we started heading in this direction, we wanted to step outside of what it is that Green Day is known for. When we think of our heroes, all are known for certain records, like, for me it is the Stones' Beggars Banquet. I want to see my band synonymous with good music, not with just one song. We wanted to explore maximum song structure and... there is an obvious political overtone, which sets the political climate for the main character. We really made it a point in the writing of this record to maintain the relationships between characters and leave it open-ended enough for people to jump in anywhere and not feel lost in some story, and be able to claim it as their own."

The American Idiot phenomenon had also reached deep into the band-members, it seemed, as well as the fanbase, allowing them to view their careers objectively: "Really good careers have peaks and valleys. We are on a peak right now. For us, this record stands alone. It is not a progression like our other records. You can see the progression in those other records. That alone makes this record somewhat monumental to this point... The average person finds themselves afraid. We are living in an information age right now, but all this information is like a tornado of bullshit. There's falsified news, reality TV, and throw in this war in Iraq on top that nobody knows why we are in it, with product placement in between. It's time to say 'Enough'! Everything turns into debate immediately. With a song like 'American Idiot', or this CD's political overtones, there's no

agenda so much as, 'I feel disenfranchised and misrepresented, and I'm tired of it'. Maybe it will open a discussion again and get back to what politics starts as, and that is open discussion."

So how have the band-members themselves coped with all the adulation? Have they grown into sensible humans at last? Not the drummer, it seems, who says "Aw, fuck, no! Matured, maybe, but not grown up. I don't have a hairy body yet. I'm still the guinea pig if there are any drugs thrown onstage. Then again, I could say I've grown up a little because now, instead of walking through a plate glass window – like, 'Oh yeah, a plate glass window, crash!' – I'll at least say, 'Wait a minute! If I jump through that plate glass window, it's going to cut me really bad, and I'll probably spend the rest of my night getting stitched up in the hospital'. I'm Tre Cool! I'm not going to step down from a gig like this, y'know? Being a drumhead got me where I am now, so I'll stay a drumhead until I die." But then he is a dad nowadays – he has two children called Frankito and Ramona – so perhaps fatherhood will mellow Tre in the end...

Mike has also become a father (to a daughter, Estelle) and co-owns a diner named Rudy's Can't Fail Café in Emeryville, California. Has he calmed down too? "I think we have changed a lot," he recently said. "People say, 'You're more mature', or whatever, but I think we're just more experienced at everything. We've learned to approach songwriting from a multitude of directions now, not just from just one source. There are no rules to this band. I feel the longer this band goes, the more we explore new avenues. We love challenging ourselves. If we are afraid of something – if it scares us – I think we're probably onto something good. We definitely come from a certain element, and we have a certain idea of what we like. We definitely carry our morals, our ideals, our ethics, and everything with us from where we come from. But I can't say I am the same person as I was five years ago. I'd be kidding myself to be that person. I think the most important thing you can do is to be honest with yourself."

He went on: "I mean, we make music for people who want to hear our music and we make music for ourselves. Ultimately what it comes down to for us is whether we please ourselves and write good songs. Call us greedy. Call us selfish. We make music for ourselves. We don't look too far into the future. Here today, gone later today, you know? We're very happy with what we've done so far, and if we can continue to put out music that makes us happy, then I'm sure there will be a good amount of people who will like it. That would be a great place to be in five years – still playing our music and enjoying playing. As to where we want to go, well – see you when we get there."

Asked just what the hell Green Day actually was, Dirnt explained: "It's just about three people that see eye to eye musically and it's almost a life of its own. It's a weird thing. It's music that changed our lives, and if people want to listen, too, I just hope it has meaning in theirs... Musically speaking, this band doesn't come across as any sort of tough band. We never really have. There are a lot of different sides to real toughness, whether you are able to dive in and show your vulnerability, or being completely honest with yourself, whatever it is. We're very competitive on an individual level, but not against other bands. Just in life. We won't let rock and roll knock us down. We want to own it."

But it's not all roses: as Armstrong explained, his mother was a little concerned about how success would affect him: "She's kinda worried about me. She doesn't know what to think of everything. We have a hard time communicating with each other, just because I don't like to talk about it that much. So she feels like she has to walk on eggshells around me all the time... she doesn't want anything. I've asked her. She's been living in the same house for over 20 years, and she's content living there. But I did give her a trip – she went to Hawaii, her and her boyfriend. And I think travelling is really good – if you paid for someone to travel, so they can go and explore and see some things they've never seen before. But I think that's probably where I get it from. I get so content with not having much. And then you get all this stuff, all this attention, and you don't really know what to do with it. You don't know how to channel it… one thing I did do was build a home studio. So I've been recording all my friends' bands for free. I produced this band called Dead And Gone, and Social Unrest, Fetish & The Criminals. And I have this side-project called Pinhead Gunpowder – nothing's up with it right now, but we played at the beginning of '94 a few times."

But the pressure never seems to get too much for him: "I have too many reasons to stick around. One is my son and my wife. And I don't feel like I'm finished yet. I'm not done, ya know? And the beauty of it is that death is forever and your problems aren't. And that's why I'm talking about my bad shit, because you vent that, you get it off your chest and you can move on to something else. There's gotta be a positive side to all this, so you just sort of try and dig it out. Get rid of all the bad – out with the bad air, in with the good air… I thought about writing a totally sarcastic song called 'I'm So Goddamn Happy,' just talking about how happy I am. Actually, I'd like to put out a double record – I'd like to put out tons of music. But I never wanna become an egomaniac. I just wanna keep things down to earth, so I think it's really important for us to take a long break after all this stuff. We just put out two records back to back, one year after another, and now we can sit back and work on ourselves as people again. So we don't parody ourselves."

The band had now become a serious phenomenon. By 2004, Mike Dirnt had even pioneered his own instrument: "I've got a signature model out. I spent two years developing this thing and it's selling like hot cakes – it's sold like 1700 of them already. A couple of years ago I asked Fender to make me a 1951 P-Bass with a rosewood fretboard. They were all freaking out, because apparently no-one's ever made one with a rosewood fretboard before! Maple's really bright when it's milled really flat, but rosewood is really bright all the time. The '2Kb icepick-in-the-ear' sound is really bright all the time. It has a good scoop to it and all the strings are of equal volume – the whole thing has a great punch to it. And I always thought that with that neck the headstock wouldn't look so tiny, and it would balance the bass better. Like matching your shoes to your shirt, ha ha! You would never notice the balance change in a million years though, it just looks better.

"Then I added the '55 cutaway so you're not rubbing your arm on that sharp ridge, and the pickups we put in are 1959 Pro-Shop reissues, it's really hot. I used to change them out for Seymour Duncan Antiquities, and I was sceptical whether these would do it – but I put them in and they were hot right out of the box. They sounded incredible. For the bridge I've got the Badass II, which is bulletproof. And I made sure we had the right capacitors and the metal-knurled knobs, and even the tuning keys are good.

"I tell people that I built a Ford F-150 truck, only it looks like a Chevy! It's medium heavy, like a regular P-Bass. But the really fun thing is that the pickups aren't in the pick-guard – you can take the pick-guard off and paint it any colour you want and put it back on, or leave it off. A six-year-old with a Phillips screwdriver can take it over. And instead of putting my signature on it there is an embossed little star, like the one I have on my wrist, my Estelle tattoo for my daughter's name."

He's also got used to the luxury of having free gear provided for him by equipment manufacturers, who have been fighting for his attention: "Years ago I used a lot of Sunn cabinets, with some Ampegs. I've always been a big fan of Sunn stuff – I only found out a few years ago that Fender actually was Sunn! And I said to them, can you get me some amps? Fender said well, we're consolidating everything under the Fender name. So when I finished designing my bass I went to Fender HQ in Arizona and they said, you should try these amps. And I said, yeah well – because I'm at the stage now where I can pretty much afford to play whatever amp I want to play, right? – and I tried them out. It was smokin'! Me and my tech looked at each other and we were like, holy shit! It's hard to argue with an Ampeg, and I used to play Mesa/Boogie – but I was going for a different sound this time and these ones are a little more present. SVTs have a great bottom end, but sometimes they get a bit muddy. The sound is extremely clean coming out of my amps. Our guitar sounds are huge! If anything I try to cut through Billie Joe's sound. I use a light distortion pedal, and now I use a Ziggy Master Blaster plus a gain – just to give it a bit of low end to raise the hairs on people's necks when we go into a guitar

solo and the bass needs to fill out the sound a little. I use the distortion separately from the booster pedal."

What music can we expect from Green Day in the future? As always, Billie Joe isn't being specific, merely saying, "All I wanna do is just write good songs and stick to it... I never wanna be that experimental. I don't wanna get into synthesisers and shit like that... No matter what, I'm gonna be writing songs for the rest of my life. But I definitely want to be respected as a musician. Well, more as a songwriter than as a musician. I wanna be fuckin' normal, is what I wanna be. The thing is, I've seen so many freaks and so many weirdos and crazy punk rockers and drunks and junkies. But for a lot of those people being weird is easy. It's so easy to be strange – the hard thing is to try to be normal. There's no such thing as normal, ya know."

Armstrong remains the most mysterious of the band, rarely explaining himself in detail in interviews. As he says, "I don't like justifying myself. We're musicians. We're not really meant to answer questions. I always thought they were a way for someone to see the other side of the band, or a side they don't already know besides the music... but we keep getting asked all these weird questions!"

He's always been a contemplative man, saying at one stage: "I didn't even know what I wanted back then. I really didn't. I didn't know if I wanted to be huge, totally successful. I never knew that. I was struggling so hard even to sign that fucking contract – when I was sitting there, I was contemplating, 'Should I just run outta here right now? Am I making the biggest mistake of my life?' A lot of people say, 'You're totally disillusioned with what money can do for people,' but money never meant shit to me. There's something very passionate to me, very romantic, about living on the street in a lot of ways. Just because I really like my lifestyle back then. I was totally content, in retrospect. A lot of it has to do with the fame... what a lot of people don't understand is that we're a band that's been around a lot longer than people know. And that's the thing. The difference between this and what happened between Kerplunk! and Dookie – in a year, I got married, I had a kid, and I sold 11 million records worldwide. That can do something to you, you know?"

But Armstrong seems to have his head screwed on despite the band's vast recent success: "I don't take any of our success for granted: if people like a song and they relate to it, that's more than I ever asked for. The only thing I can keep doing is being myself, being a songwriter. I'm not a politician telling people what to do, I even have trouble thinking of myself as a musician sometimes... I don't know what the word 'punk' means anymore. To me, it's always had more to do with the old Clint Eastwood line 'Do you feel lucky, punk?' It's all just rock'n'roll."

Nostalgia plays a part in his outlook, as it does for most people: "Sometimes I think it'd be cool to just hang out with my friends, drink beer, smoke cigarettes. The more I think about it, the more I'd be really happy with that... There was this certain rock'n'roll underdog thing that we always had – we always drove for something, always drove from town to town in a small van. And you know, I fuckin' like touring like that – it's like culture shock, really, driving around in a van, setting up my amp when I get there, and playing. That's rock'n'roll, that's what it started out as. A bunch of sweaty pigs in some tiny fuckin' bar having a hootenanny, that's what punk rock was to me, that's what drove me to it. I love rock music in its simplest, rawest form. And I think we're the only band, really, that plays rock'n'roll... When I come up to friends I haven't talked to in a while, there's a weirdness. And the ones who are really close to me don't really bring up anything, but that thing is still there; it's still in the air. And sometimes I'll just not say anything the whole time we're hanging out. I'll be totally quiet, because the only thing I'll have to talk about is my band, and I get so sick of talking about my band and myself. So I'll just be quiet, since that's the only thing there is to me, except for my son and my wife."

He still has ambitions for Green Day ("When people say, my favourite band is The Who, you know they're talking about a classic rock band. I want people to talk about Green Day like that") but knows that he can react negatively to attention: "I think that when rock stars get pretty big, a lot of them go way deep inside themselves and shut out the world. That's sort of what happened to me. I became disconnected with what was going on. That's what this record is about, about channelling my anger and my angst into things that are really important. Trying to try to find something that comes out of it that's positive."

"I enjoy the fact that I'm misunderstood most of the time," he added. "That's fine. That's what keeps people guessing. As long as people are still talking and arguing about you, then you're still some kind of threat. I don't want to tell people what to do or think – I just want them to think."

But of one thing Armstrong was clear, although this would seem strange in the light of recent releases: "We're not a political band and we don't want to tell people what to do or what to think. We just want to tell them to think. If they're not happy they should get up and do something, even if it turns out that they did the wrong thing. At least they know they've tried and making mistakes is a lot better than not doing anything."

Looking back on the long and turbulent career of his band, Armstrong is philosophical, explaining: "In a way everything just happened in our career. We were a couple of guys with shitty jobs – if we had jobs for long enough – playing in a band, having fun, recording an album and all of a sudden things took off. Punk went from being unpopular to absolutely popular!

Of course, we were having fun. Of course, we did a couple of outrageous things. Who wouldn't? But you reach a point in your life where you ask yourself 'Is it all I want to do?' And then you have to decide.

"Just because we're a bit older doesn't mean we've become boring. We have different values and let's face facts, I'm a family man. It's a lot harder to be on tour and just live it up when you've got a family. A family means responsibility."

On the subject of family – he has two sons – Billie is, like his bandmates, aware of the life-changing responsibilities that it carries. "I never thought I'd say it, but I do miss my family more than I thought when I'm on the road. I still like being on stage and I'm a musician. To be honest, I couldn't be anything else. I don't qualify for much else, but I still miss them... Of course, I could take them along, but it wouldn't really be fair. Being on tour is a lot of stress and I wouldn't have much time for them. So it's better for them if they're in their environment with their mom and friends. How much fun can it be for a kid to be on tour without any other kids to play with? To have different time zones, get up at odd hours because you have a schedule to keep, no other kids around and everybody's really busy because things have to get done?"

Billie Joe, who had his first child in his early twenties, knows this more than most, attempting to reconcile the touring and fathering lifestyle with little success. As he said, "I realised that for Joey, the rock and roll touring life is not a good atmosphere for a kid. I tried to make it to where it would be, bringing lots of his toys out. But there are no familiar surroundings for him. And he likes all the attention – people come up and say hello to him every day, people who are on tour with us. But he doesn't have his own room or a home to go to every day. So, no more touring for Joey... it's so hard to be a father and a musician at the same time. If I get into one thing and I pay close attention to it, like if I'm with Joey and I start neglecting my music, then I feel like I should play more often. So I start playing my music, and then I'm going, 'Am I neglecting Joey?' So it becomes hard to do everything at the same time."

"I wanna create a very mellow and sound atmosphere for him," he added, "because I don't wanna make any mistakes for him – I want him to be able to make his own mistakes. And even when it comes to swearing, I don't cuss in front of my kid. I'd rather him get it from some dirty-mouthed kid at school. Then at least I'd know, I could go 'Thank God – my kid is in a real world and he's learning these things from his surroundings.' That'd be a good thing. Because the best things you ever learn are the things you learn in kindergarten."

Armstrong has learned much along the way, it seems, not least about himself: "Oh, I was an angry, pessimistic and egomaniac person. Sometimes if I look at my old lyrics, they seem to be full of rage but still empty. There was an emptiness in my life. Now I'm trying to fill that void… It doesn't mean that you have

to bottle up all your anger and your rage, but I learned that it makes a lot more sense to find out what really makes you angry, then try and channel the anger and to try to remove the cause for it. I think it's your own choice if you turn from an angry young man to a bitter, old bastard, or if you stay angry in a good way."

Perhaps acting roles will come to Green Day, now that they're famous? No. As Dirnt laughs, "A role in The Simpsons? I'll leave that to the Red Hot Chili Peppers. It's a funny show but I wouldn't want to market myself in that direction."

"I don't like actors," adds Billie Joe. "And I hate other musicians, except for the ones that I already knew or the few that are cool. I don't want to become an actor and I'm insulted when actors become musicians. I'm just not into the whole rubbing shoulders with the big boys kind of thing. I'm doing just fine without them."

As the youngest of six children, Billie Joe didn't have too many fond memories of childhood, and seems keen not to repeat the mistakes his mother made. "I'm the epitome of a latchkey kid," he said: "By the time my mom, who had me when she was 40, got around to raising me, she was like, 'You do what you want, I'm sick of being strict all the time'." Applying this to his own son, he explained: "The last thing I want for Joey is for him to be known as my son. I'd rather keep the magazines and the fame away from him. Which will be impossible, but I think it's really important for him to develop his own identity. Let him make his own mistakes. I'd rather be the station-wagon kind of parent, you know, like going to Wally World. I just want to be a normal dad. Being a parent is the hardest thing I've ever had to do in my whole life. I'm totally self-conscious all the time, making sure I don't scream in front of Joey, trying to keep some sort of comfortable atmosphere for him. I'm not used to that. I'm usually like 'arrrgghh!'... I'm trying to keep up my end of the bargain. It takes two, you know, a mom and a dad.

Adrienne's an amazing mom. Mothers have got the worst jobs in the whole world. And I never realised that until I had a kid. I don't care what you do, or what job you complain about. Try to be a mother. You won't last a fucking day."

As we go to press, Green Day have released a live album and DVD from the American Idiot tour titled Bullet In A Bible. These are documents of the over-the-top live extravaganza that their live shows have become, bolstered by second guitarist Jason White of The Deviants and including a section in which members of the crowd are called up to perform a cover of the old Gilman Street-era classic, 'Knowledge' by Operation Ivy. Of the live experience, Mike said: "Playing the new record front to back really works live. Right now we're playing big segments of the record, but we're also playing a lot of the old stuff. Our set averages about an hour 45 minutes, but we can easily play for four hours. We're turning into the punk rock Bruce Springsteen! Our show is all about maximum impact. I wish I could see my band live... I'll never be able to see Green Day live, and that sucks!"

Has any band ever made such an outrageous comeback? Well, it's arguable – you might look at Madonna, Kylie Minogue and Blur, all of whom came back from career doldrums in their mid-career to enormous adulation. But none have done so with such vast commercial figures – the numbers say it all in Green Day's case. Crucially, can they repeat this feat on the next album, or even maintain their progress at or near the very top of the rock tree? Only time will tell.

NEAR THE END OF '93, GREEN DAY DID THE UNTHINKABLE: THEY SIGNED TO MAJOR LABEL, REPRISE RECORDS, RECORDED DOOKIE— AN ALBUM NAMED AFTER DOG TURDS, CLIMBED INTO AN EX-TRAVELING LIBRARY CALLED THE BOOKMOBILE, TOURED THE WORLD, GAINED MILLIONS OF FANS WORLWIDE, AND PLAYED WOODSTOCK '94— A FEST THAT CATERED TO 100,000 SOILED HIPPIES. .....TOTALLY WEIRD.

FOLLOWING DOOKIE, GREEN DAY TOURED, GOT MARRIED, HAD BABIES, AND TOURED MORE— IN SUPPORT OF THEIR NEXT TWO ALBUMS— 1995'S INSOMNIAC, AND 1997'S NIMROD. OCCASIONALLY, THE BAND WOULD LOSE IT— AND ALL HELL WOULD BREAK LOSE— AS IT DID IN 97, AT A FREE TOWER RECORDS SHOW IN NYC.

THIS ISNT LOVE & PEACE, ITS FUCKING ANARCHY!

CONTINUED ON PAGE 11

TRACK-BY-TRACK ANALYSIS

This song-by-song run-through of Green Day's recorded catalogue seeks to provide a clear, unbiased assessment of each of their songs and albums. Where a song is included more than once – on a single, live album or compilation as well as the parent album – I have indicated as such and referred the reader to the original entry.

Furthermore, with singles and live / compilation albums I haven't annotated each track, summing up the content with an overview: fuller analysis is reserved for original studio albums.

I've focused only on UK releases – which means that the 1980s EPs on the Skene! label are reviewed as part of the 1039/ Smoothed Out Happy Hours compilation CD in 1990 – as Green Day product from Japan, the USA and other territories came in variant formats and tracklistings.

I've given each song and album a rating out of five as follows:

★ ★ ★ ★ ★ Absolutely essential

★ ★ ★ ★ Excellent

★ ★ ★ Average

★ ★ Poor

★ Terrible

Tom King

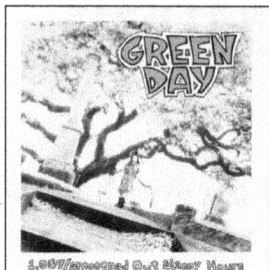

1,039 / SMOOTHED OUT SLAPPY HOURS

(Album, 1990)

Tracklisting: At The Library / Don't Leave Me / I Was There / Disappearing Boy / Green Day / Going To Pasalacqua / 16 / Road To Acceptance / Rest / The Judge's Daughter / Paper Lanterns / Why Do You Want Him? / 409 In Your Coffeemaker / Knowledge / 1,000 Hours / Dry Ice / Only Of You / The One I Want / I Want To Be Alo3ne

At The Library ★ ★

"What is it about you that I adore?" warbles Billie Joe Armstrong, touchingly but untunefully, on this simple bit of punk-by-numbers that features almost demo-quality guitars and vocals. John Kiffmeyer's drums are more or less on point – although the tempo could be faster and the attack harsher – but come on, they were still practically (sweet) children at this stage…

Don't Leave Me ★ ★

A slight tale of paranoia and fear about being abandoned, 'Don't Leave Me' boasts some surprisingly mellow arpeggioed guitars (were Green Day ever just a punk band, you wonder?) although Billie Joe's awful vocals and lyrics leave everything to be desired. Is that a touch of Johnny Rotten-style sneer in his vocals, or did the pressure of recording in a matter of minutes before the budget ran out just make him irritable?

I Was There ★ ★

Still only in his late teens, Billie Joe comes across as somewhat pretentious with world-weary lines such as "Looking back upon my life / And the places that I've been / Pictures, faces, girls I've loved…", and the strained vocals of 'I Was There' make it slightly painful to listen to. And yet he's trying to dig into deeper territory than merely punk outrage, asking himself "I sometimes wonder what I can give" with perception that most kids of his age lack.

Disappearing Boy ★ ★ ★
A classic Green Day tale of disorientation, 'Disappearing Boy' deals with Billie Joe's insecurity as he walks into a room full of strangers – punk with a grunge ethos? The backing vocals are horribly flat but the tinny guitars are punkishly entertaining and the song bodes well for the future. Don't expect sophistication though – the low budget environment strains through every note.

Green Day ★ ★ ★
"I picture someone, I think it's you / You're standing so damn close / My body begins to swell" warbles Billie Joe unattractively at the start of this account of a stoner session. But the song isn't as gurningly appreciative of the herbal experience as you might expect from this stage in Green Day's career: rather, the song is uncertain and slightly paranoid, giving the lie to Billie Joe's assertion that at this stage in their careers, Green Day couldn't ask intelligent questions.

Going To Pasalacqua ★ ★
More teenage angst from Billie Joe as the band churn out this accurately executed elegy to midnight sleeplessness. The stop-start riff, on which the band come together with remarkable precision for such young musicians, and the punk power chords which follow it, are pretty reasonable examples of the band's emerging musicianship.

16 ★
'16' is basically more of the same 'Going To Pasalacqua'-style teen stuff, with amateurish lines such as "I wish my youth would forever last / Why are these times so unfair" not exactly tripping

off Billie Joe's youthful tongue. In fact, the song itself is highly skippable, with its ascending chord sequence and vocal line a little too shrill to listen to with anything but mild annoyance – unless you're a seriously devoted fan.

Road To Acceptance ★

"Adolescence" kind of rhymes with "Just can't make sense", granted, but that's the only remotely cunning thing about 'Road To Acceptance', which falls apart at its end without having achieved much. Listen out for some slightly funky bass fills from Mike Dirnt, though – the least obvious presence on this record so far, due to the super-weak production.

Rest ★

Avoid 'Rest', it's terrible. The slow tom-tom drumming from Kiffmeyer and the reasonably adroit guitar arpeggios aren't the problem – it's the caterwauled, utterly out of tune vocals that make the song unlistenable. Billie Joe was showing clear promise as a songwriter with a knack for crafted melodies, so why the band didn't tune down to allow him to hit the notes on the line "Angel... angel" is a mystery.

The Judge's Daughter ★ ★ ★

This song is more interesting: Billie Joe pipes extensively about his unrequited love for a "princess" who bumps into him on the street, before asking "the being in the sky that my parents told me of" for guidance. Needless to say, none is forthcoming, and the ending is left ambiguous. It's deep stuff for a young band, and promising – even if most of the sentiments on the next album avoided such attempts at profundity altogether.

Paper Lanterns ★ ★

Punk by the numbers, 'Paper Lanterns' has some moderately engaging lines in "So when are all my troubles going to end? / I'm understanding now that / We are only friends" but still doesn't quite work – it's another attempt at depth which is let down by the ridiculous sound and vocals. And the band had been paying too much attention to 80s hardcore bands like Black Flag, without actually taking on any of those bands' strengths.

Why Do You Want Him? ★ ★

Perhaps the most generic of the early Green Day songs, 'Why Do You Want Him?' lifts into an ascending chorus and boasts vocal melodies aplenty, even if they aren't quite accurate...

409 In Your Coffeemaker ★ ★

Here Billie Joe looks back in frustration over what appears to be a litany of wasted opportunities, although he's not being specific – preferring to focus on how he's sitting in a haze, the slacker generation epitomised. Musically, the band are sitting squarely in Gilman Street-style homemade punk territory, although there are touches of studio trickery such as a delayed vocal line from time to time which at least prove that someone is sitting in the control room.

Knowledge ★ ★ ★

Operation Ivy's 'Knowledge' – something of a 'Stairway To Heaven' or 'Ace Of Spades' to the Gilman Street generation – is surprisingly fragile, with hardly anything to the song other than a ska-style rhythm and the anthemic wail of 'All I know is that I don't know nothin''. Its simple, nihilistic sentiments are the perfect expression of apathy for a whole demographic of teenagers – a demonstration of which is the song's popularity to this day.

1,000 Hours ★ ★

Like some acne-ridden Romeo serenading a trailer-trash Juliet, Billie Joe wails out a tinny ode of love: "Our romance / Is a love trance / And now we'll never part / 1,000 hours / Of such a love shower". The words don't really scan – you can hear him stumbling while trying to fit them all in – but there's a certain stupid, puppyish charm to the song that is universes away from the sophistication, in sound and sentiment, of the later albums.

Dry Ice ★ ★ ★

A highly catchy pop-punk riff with soaring vocals pulls in the listener with immediate effect on this high point of the 1,000 Hours EP. Although it's still not anywhere near as cool as, say, 'Basket Case', the song does have its own merits – primarily a lovelorn tone that makes you smile. "Come ease the pain that's in my heart," warbles Armstrong, who must have just been dumped by his high-school sweetheart.

Only Of You ★

Truly demo-like in composition and structure, 'Only Of You' sounds like a pack of 14-year-olds after too much sugar and tartrazine. It's a love song again – and this time a truly feeble one. "If I could only hold you / It's the only thing I want to do" rhymes Billie Joe, causing a generation of punk fans variously to fall over in laughter or reach for the sick bag…

The One I Want ★ ★

More lovey lyrics ("Now you know how I feel / This love is forever") but couched in a song that actually provides a bit of musical satisfaction. This time there's a clear and catchy pattern that hooks the listener in – and still repays repeated listens despite the cheesy lyrics and the foul production.

I Want To Be Alone ★ ★ ★

The album ends with – at last – a brattish, angry tune in which Armstrong simply asks to be left alone in his room with his thoughts. Is it aimed at his parents? At his teachers? Who knows, but it's a decent bit of protest whatever its target.

Conclusion

This collection of early Green Day EPs may be inconsistent

and downright weak in parts, but it should be borne in mind that the compilation wasn't designed to be a competitive part of their catalogue – more of a reminder and keepsake for the most dedicated fans of their idols' early days. Regard it as a souvenir, and be grateful that some rapacious record company hasn't snapped up the EPs and put them out as a series of full-price CDs.

Overall rating: ★ ★

KERPLUNK!
(Album, 17 January 1992)

Tracklisting: 2000 Light Years Away / One For The Razorbacks / Welcome To Paradise / Christie Road / Private Ale / Dominated Love Slave / One Of My Lies / 80 / Android / No One Knows / Who Wrote Holden Caulfield / Words I Might Have Ate / Sweet Children / Best Thing In Town / Strangeland / My Generation

2000 Light Years Away ★ ★ ★
"'Cause she's 2000 light years away," intones Billie Joe dreamily, as Kerplunk! – a far more deftly-executed and performed album than the EPs which had preceded it – takes off. This song is a great opener, neither as heavy as later tunes nor so pensive in its subject matter that listeners are prevented from easing gently into the record. Note the cheeky Pistols homage in the ascending semitone slide that the guitars execute during each chorus.

One For The Razorbacks ★ ★ ★
A moderately entertaining song that, for once, doesn't suffer from flat backing vocals (some tuning had obviously been going on). This makes all the difference: the tale of Juliet ("Juliet's crying cause now she's realising love can be / Filled

with pain and distrust") is actually an upbeat, encouraging tale in which Armstrong offers to help her regain her feet. The little Samaritan...

Welcome To Paradise ★ ★ ★ ★

The first bona fide Green Day classic, 'Welcome To Paradise' is a tale of urban squalor told in diary form by Billie Joe to his mother. As he warns, "Dear mother / Can you hear me whining? / It's been three whole weeks / Since I have left your home / This sudden fear has left me trembling..." – leading into a song boasting an expert chorus and some funky fills from Dirnt.

Christie Road ★ ★

"Take me to the tracks at Christie Road" pleads Armstrong – was this a real location for a peaceful refuge in his childhood, or just a figment of his imagination? Either way, it sounds like a pleasant place to be, with his boredom "smoked away" and an escape from the pressures that plagued him. His falsetto squeals from time to time are lively, too.

Private Ale ★ ★

Fast, semi-furious and showcasing Armstrong's powerful grasp of a power chord, 'Private Ale' is a filler song but not bad for all that. It's more of the punk by the numbers that the band had shown that they could write already, and no doubt a better song live than on record.

Dominated Love Slave ★ ★

Sick humour in a hillbilly style was hardly the expected direction here, but it works well. Tre handles vocals on a ridiculous barn-dance stomp, banjos and all, with the immortal lines "'Cause I love feelin' dirty / And I love feelin' cheap / And I love it when you hurt me / So drive them staples deep..."

One Of My Lies ★ ★

Billie Joe gets profound on this slight but entertaining stomper, in which he asks eternal questions such as "Why does my life have to be so small? / Yet death is forever", perhaps in answer to the silliness of the previous song. It works, though, and indicates that behind the endless japes and fooling around, the little round-shouldered guy's brain is working overtime.

80 ★ ★ ★

A proto-'Basket Case' – with its lyrics dealing with mental instability ("Sometimes I wonder if I should be left alone / And lock myself up in a padded room / I'd sit and spew my guts out to the open air"), '80' is the first sign that Green Day felt the need to express their paranoia to the world. It's fairly good stuff too, an upbeat, pounding punk anthem.

Android ★ ★ ★

"It seems so frightening," muses Billie Joe, "Time passes by like lightning / Before you know it you're struck down / I always waste my time on my chemical emotions / It keeps my head spinning around"… Musically unremarkable but lyrically astute, in 'Android' Green Day address the subject of ageing and shifts in perspective – neither normally the province of punk nor pop. The subject of Armstrong's fear of a short life seems to be at the forefront – what a thinker the boy was turning out to be…

No One Knows ★ ★

Another piece of amped-up miserablism from Green Day, 'No One Knows' sees Billie Joe piping "I see my friends begin to age / A short countdown to what end" in further contemplation of life taking its course. It's a slow, power-chord scrub and builds to a finish aided by more layered vocals – increasingly a Green Day trademark.

Who Wrote Holden Caulfield ★ ★

A frantic bit of semi-hardcore about an unnamed "boy who fogs this world" and in all other ways resembles the titular JD

Salinger anti-hero, 'Who Wrote Holden Caulfield' is as lively as Green Day get on Kerplunk!. Nonetheless, the slightly weak production makes the song less weighty than it could, and should, have been.

Words I Might Have Ate ★ ★ ★ ★

For many the high point of the album, 'Words I Might Have Ate' is an acoustic strum with jaunty, almost Kinks-like dual vocals that is both well-executed and expertly written. The lyrics – "Now I dwell on what you remind me of / A sweet young girl who sacrificed her love" – are the standard Armstrong naiveties of the era, but the song's a success anyway.

Sweet Children ★ ★

What appears to be a simple paean to childhood innocence – "Sweet children, remember when?" – and is of course named after (or before) the pre-Green Day band's title, has some dark undertones ("Putting his hand on her thigh / Ability has now been ripped") in typical style. It works moderately well, although the band would perfect this kind of cheerful-but-grim elegy later on.

Best Thing In Town ★ ★

A strange glimpse into some alternate reality or other overlaid by a weird, almost rockabilly guitar break, 'Best Thing In Town' is one of the oddest songs Green Day have ever recorded. The slightly eeries lyrics don't reveal much, but once again Armstrong seems to be in something of a youthful trance…

Strangeland ★ ★

Over a droned, one-note punk fretboard-scrub, Armstrong intones the chummy words of "Get in my mind and you will find / Mother love from all mankind" before a funky, stop-start motif that belies Green Day's superficial youthful innocence. There's songwriting genius deep down inside, it appears.

My Generation ★ ★

A by-the-numbers cover of the Who standard amped up with some punky shouts, the sound of smashing glass and the interesting device of sharing the original bass solo between all three members, 'My Generation' is a bit of fluffy fun that does no harm and doesn't need to be played twice.

Conclusion

The first 'real' Green Day album is almost as inconsistent as the EPs which preceded it, but promises much for the future in the two or three songs that stand out. Ironically, the standard punk thrash seems to be second nature to them now: what elevates Green Day from the popcore pack is their grasp on songs such as 'Words I Might Have Ate', which depart radically from that particular old saw. The verdict? Could, and would, do better.

Overall rating: ★ ★

BASKET CASE
(Single, 20 August 1994, Reissued 29 January 1995)

Tracklisting: Basket Case / Longview (Live) / Burnout (Live) / 2000 Light Years Away (Live)

A flop on its first issue but a deservedly massive hit the second time around, 'Basket Case' – and its superb video – could have been paired up with any song as a single and it would still have gone down in history as a cultural event. Play it and remember a simpler era in pop, rock, punk, whatever you want to call it…

Overall rating: ★ ★ ★ ★ ★

WELCOME TO PARADISE

(Single, 29 October 1994)

Tracklisting: Welcome To Paradise / Chump / Emenius Sleepus

When 'Basket Case' failed to provide the success that Warners wanted for Green Day on its first release, it was hoped that one of the album's other high points would deliver the goods – and so it did. 'Welcome To Paradise' was unforgettable, with its catchy riff and miserablist lyrics the perfect entrée to the Green Day point of view. Paired with two Dookie standards, it was a memorable way in to the pop-punk canon.

Overall rating: ★ ★ ★

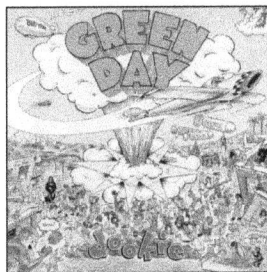

DOOKIE

(Album, 5 November 1994)

Tracklisting: Burnout / Having A Blast / Chump / Longview / Welcome To Paradise / Pulling Teeth / Basket Case / She / Sassafras Roots / When I Come Around / Coming Clean / Emenius Sleepus / In The End / F.O.D.

Burnout ★ ★ ★

Boasting a spanking new sound, all crisp treble and warm bass, Dookie kicks off with 'Burnout', a sneering chunk of bile that serves the album perfectly. Where the grunge icons had wailed of their misery, Armstrong offered up a darker, less angsty take on it all: "I'm not growing up / I'm just burning out / And I stepped in line / to walk amongst the dead" he repeats, providing an introduction to the masses that many would never forget.

Having A Blast ★ ★ ★

Superficially a bad joke (the subject is a terrorist, set to self-destruct, who warns "I'm taking all you down with me /

Explosives duct-taped to my spine / Nothing's gonna change my mind") this song is scary and plain intimidating. Armstrong sings the worryingly nihilistic lyrics in a disturbingly rational voice, telling the tale of a wasted life that cares not a jot for anyone else.

Chump ★ ★

Armstrong lets out more repressed anger on 'Chump', on which he peels out a litany of anger against another anonymous subject: "I don't know you / But I think I hate you / You're the reason for my misery". Whether the songwriting sessions for Dookie were particularly grim is not known, but it's obvious that thoughts of rage, depression and paranoia were at the forefront of the writers' minds from time to time…

Longview ★ ★ ★ ★

A classic Green Day tale of everyday boredom – there's nothing on TV, no-one is calling on the phone, jerking off has become dull and parents are just a drag – 'Longview' has been a feature of the live set for years. The fanbase immediately identified with lines like "I'm sick of all the same old shit / In a house with unlocked doors / And I'm fucking lazy", of course. It was all a long way from the conceptual American Idiot, that's for sure.

Welcome To Paradise ★ ★ ★ ★

The re-recorded 'Welcome To Paradise' from Kerplunk! is obviously, like the earlier version, an excellent piece of songwriting that hooks the listener in with great nonchalance. The new recording is warmer, tighter and better executed, with excellent backing vocals that descend like so many classic rock songs from the last few decades.

Pulling Teeth ★ ★ ★ ★

'Pulling Teeth' is hilarious – a tale of a man imprisoned by

his kidnapper lover. There's not much to the song other than a topline melody which sticks brilliantly in the listener's head, but that alone is more than so many other punk bands of the day were providing. A rarely-mentioned high point of this excellent album, 'Pulling Teeth' is that rare thing – an album track that is not filler.

Basket Case ★ ★ ★ ★ ★
The highlight of the entire Green Day catalogue for many, 'Basket Case' transcends the pop-punk genre to enter the rock pantheon as one of the best songs ever written. It's short, incandescent, endlessly hummable and slyly intelligent: when Billie Joe whinges, "Do you have the time, to listen to me whine?" he's commenting on literally everything – the fans, the band, the song, the industry... Sheer genius.

She ★ ★ ★
More exploration of social alienation comes with 'She', in which Billie Joe plugs directly into the mindset of his listeners with lyrics like "Are you locked up in a world / That's been planned out for you? / Are you feeling like a social tool without a use?" The slacker generation bought right into this kind of half-hearted protest with enthusiasm, helped by the song's upbeat sounds and the glistening production.

Sassafras Roots ★ ★
This time the theme is of waste – a word that Billie Joe repeats endlessly throughout the song. A funky bass part from Dirnt gives this oddly-titled tune some sparkle, although it isn't one of Dookie's high points. Still, the concept of rejected awkwardness is spelled out with passion, which counts for much...

When I Come Around ★ ★
Lines such as "You may find out that your self-doubt means nothing was ever there" may seem sage, but 'When I Come

Around' is more notable for its hooky chorus riff, a rarity in the often punk-by-numbers world of Green Day (not that anyone was complaining, as the album went several times platinum).

Coming Clean ★ ★ ★
Billie Joe, known more for his words than his guitar performance, comes across well on 'Coming Clean'. The usually raucous guitar sounds more thoughtful and layered on this expert piece of pop songsmithery, in which – with a touch of nostalgia – Billie warbles "Seventeen and coming clean for the first time / I finally figured out myself for the first time / I found out what it takes to be a man" with an almost serious tone.

Emenius Sleepus ★ ★
It's Dirnt's chance to execute a freaky, funky moment, as his bass clicks away behind the riffage in 'Emenius Sleepus'. The story of a friend who had changed beyond all recognition, this song is another in a series from Armstrong, whose lyrical obsession with ageing and the passing of time has cropped up in a dozen songs before this one.

In The End ★ ★
A malevolent farewell to an unidentified person who "got what you want / Someone to look good with and light your cigarette / Is this what you really want?", 'In The End' promises over a frantic backing – Tre is on particularly ebullient form – that there will be no redemption when all is said and done.

F.O.D. ★ ★ ★
A mostly acoustic track to kiss off the album, 'F.O.D.' (a polite way of saying 'Fuck off and die') is, like the Oasis song 'Married With Children' – the epilogue song on their album Definitely Maybe, released the same year – a quiet, thoughtful way of completing this rather violent album. When Billie Joe sings "You're just a fuck / I can't explain it 'cause I think you

suck / I'm taking pride in telling you to fuck off and die", you know he means it.

Conclusion
Dookie was where Green Day found their niche. Their newly-polished pop-punk sound was the perfect antidote to post-Cobain grunge culture, and – aided by some career-best songwriting from Armstrong – was almost inevitably going to be a massive hit. And massive it was, springboarding sky-high off the ridiculously catchy 'Basket Case'. The future looked bright… the future looked Green.

Overall rating: ★ ★ ★ ★

LONGVIEW
(Single, 18 March 1995)

Tracklisting: Longview / On The Wagon / F.O.D. (Live)

Even easier to digest in single format than on its parent album, 'Longview' and its irked-teen themes paved the way admirably for more post-Dookie success. 'On The Wagon' – a typically peeved Armstrong composition of the day – and a live version of 'F.O.D.' were worth the purchase price too.

Overall rating: ★ ★ ★

WHEN I COME AROUND
(Single, 20 May 1995)

Tracklisting: When I Come Around / Longview (Live) / Burnout (Live) / 2000 Light Years Away (Live)

Bitter as it was, 'When I Come Around' was an appropriate reminder that beneath the punkish gurning lay a band with serious resentment. Armstrong's anger at his unspecified but fickle target gave the song serious power, especially when tied up with these three live tracks – ample instances of the band's live capabilities.

Overall rating: ★ ★ ★

INSOMNIAC
(Album, 21 October 1995)

Tracklisting: Armatage Shanks / Brat / Stuck With Me / Geek / Stink Breath / No Pride / Babs Uvula Who? / 86 / Panic Song / Stuart And The Ave. / Brain Stew / Jaded / Westbound Sign / Tight Wad Hill / Walking Contradiction

Armatage Shanks ★ ★ ★
"I'm a loner in a catastrophic mind" are the first words of the much-anticipated follow-up album to the vast-selling Dookie. It's a relatively hard-hitting song, with Dirnt's fat bass line pushing it along in one of his more inventive performances.

Brat ★ ★ ★
The amusing tale of a callous young individual who is waiting for his parents to die and bequeath their fortune ("Mom and Dad don't look so hot these days / They're getting over the hill / Death is closing in and catching up / As far as I can tell"), 'Brat' is a simple mockery of the rich kids that were the perennial targets of the punk crowd.

Stuck With Me ★ ★
One of the first overtly political songs that Billie Joe had written, 'Stuck With Me' mentions all the standard devices that cropped up in the first wave of UK punk almost two decades before – the class system, the elite and so on. Armstrong wails:

"Class structure waving colours / Bleeding from my throat / Not subservient to you I'm just alright / Downclassed by the powers that be" – despite the US punk scene being quite a different beast to its Transatlantic counterpart.

Geek Stink Breath ★ ★ ★

A mid-tempo classic that became a Green Day standard, 'Geek Stink Breath' is an attack on the speed users who populated the band's environs. Billie hisses "A slow progression / Killing my complexion / And it's rotting out my teeth" and mentions the scabbed faces of those of over-use this pernicious, but cheap, plentiful and initially enjoyable substance.

No Pride ★ ★

The newfound political rage of Green Day finds an outlet in 'No Pride', in which Billie Joe sings "No culture's worth a stream of piss / Or a bullet in my face" with surprising vehemence – although career-long observers can draw a distinct line between the early days of Insomniac and American Idiot thanks to overt tunes such as this one, in which the band are more specific than usual about their targets.

Babs Uvula Who? ★ ★

Enough of the bile – 'Babs Uvula Who?' is a piece of meaningless fun centred on the exquisite harmonies on segments of lines such as the "all wound up" in "I've got a knack for fucking everything up / My temper flies and I get myself all wound up". Here the band are mocking uptight people, it seems, although they're also noting how irritating life can be. Listen out for more inventive stuff from Mike.

86 ★ ★ ★

Is it fashion victims or all-round musical snobs that Billie Joe is lampooning in '86' with lines such as "So stand aside and let the next one pass / Don't let the door kick you in the ass"? Warning that there's no return from '86, and adding "Don't even try!" the singer makes it clear that hangers-on to the notion that those times were better aren't welcome around these parts.

Panic Song ★ ★
There's little fun to be had with 'Panic Song', in which the band generate a tense intro composed of feedback and Dirnt's jittery bass. Singing "The world is a sick machine / Breeding a mass of shit" and other cheery lines, Armstrong makes it clear that something's bothering him, although he doesn't specify what.

Stuart And The Ave. ★ ★
Laughing bitterly as his lost love drives away, Armstrong mocks himself: "I'm beat down and half brain dead / The long lost king of fools / I may be dumb / But I'm not stupid enough to stay with you". Whether the split the narrator experiences is real or fictional is not explained, but it's not pretty either way.

Brain Stew ★ ★
With an almost heavy rock riff akin to Led Zeppelin or AC/DC, 'Brain Stew' is a lumbering, paranoiac elegy, with Armstrong intoning "My eyes feel like they're gonna bleed / Dried up and bulging out my skull" in grisly horror-freak fashion. It's a powerful song, much contrasted by the one that follows…

Jaded ★ ★ ★
…which is the closest to hardcore punk that Green Day have yet come, with a 2/4 thrash metal drum pattern that sounds a little stilted in Tre's hands but which lends ferocity to the otherwise slightly pedestrian riff. "There is no progress", sniggers Armstrong, "Evolution killed it all / I found my place in nowhere". Jaded indeed.

Westbound Sign ★ ★ ★ ★
"She's taking off," sings Armstrong repeatedly in this expertly-crafted road song, in which a girl leaves her home town in a

cloud of dust (and "10 minute breakdowns") to seek her fortune in California. It's a simple enough song without much musical complexity, but sits perfectly amid the darker, more sophisticated tunes on this album – almost providing a touch of light relief.

Tight Wad Hill ★
With lines like "Drugstore hooligan / Another white trash mannequin / On display to rot up on the hill", it's not clear who Green Day are attacking here – but their venom is on show for all to see. Then again, there have been a few songs like this one, non-specific and not particularly memorable… we hardly require another.

Walking Contradiction ★ ★ ★
Possibly the most lyrically thoughtful and scathing song that Green Day had yet written, 'Walking Contradiction' is the tale of a "smart-ass playing dumb" who takes all and gives nothing to anyone. Who the band are referring to is not specified, as usual, but there are strong hints at the aggression to come.

Conclusion
With Insomniac Green Day both pleased and dissatisfied their fanbase. The pop-punk template – riffs with nice harmony choruses – had been established by Dookie, leaving some fans wanting more of the same and others wanting to see progression away from it. In attempting to achieve both, the band pleased few, with most people concluding that Dookie was a one-off.

Overall rating: ★ ★ ★

GEEK STINK BREATH
(Single, 7 October 1995)

Tracklisting: Geek Stink Breath / I Want To Be On TV / Don't Wanna Fall In Love

An easy score for Green Day, the 'Geek Stink Breath' single with its two B-sides (see Shenanigans) pulled in the buyers in sufficient numbers to reassure Warners that the band still retained a healthy fanbase post-Insomniac.

Overall rating: ★ ★ ★

STUCK WITH ME
(Single, 6 January 1996)

Tracklisting: Stuck With Me / When I Come Around (Live) / Jaded (Live)

Backed with two live tunes, 'Stuck With Me' – not the most cheerful of Green Day's work – was an unusual choice for a single, but one which displayed something of the depth which still remained hidden from those only familiar with 'Basket Case'.

Overall rating: ★ ★ ★

BRAIN STEW / JADED
(Single, 6 July 1996)

Tracklisting: Brain Stew / Jaded / Do Da Da / Brain Stew (Clean Radio Version)

Combining the slow, staccato 'Brain Stew' with the semi-hardcore 'Jaded' was a masterstroke, allowing fans to hear both sides of the band – the rock and the punk. The first 'clean' song that Green Day had recorded was an indication of their growing presence on mainstream radio.

Overall rating: ★ ★ ★

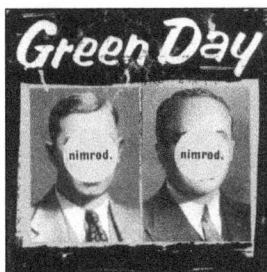

NIMROD
(Album, 25 October 1997)

Tracklisting: Nice Guys Finish Last / Hitchin' A Ride / Grouch / Redundant / Scattered / All The Time / Worry Rock / Platypus (I Hate You) / Last Ride In / Jinx / Haushinka / Walking Alone / Suffocate / Uptight / Take Back / King For A Day / Time Of Your Life (Good Riddance) / Prosthetic Head

Nice Guys Finish Last ★ ★ ★ ★

The sheer insouciant swagger of 'Nice Guys Finish Last', with its by now trademark top-line backing-vocal melody that begged you to hum it, made it one of the best openers of any Green Day record ever released. The sound is full and satisfying, and bodes well for the rest of the album.

Hitchin' A Ride ★ ★ ★

Getting high seems to be the object of the character in 'Hitchin' A Ride' – and although he says "Cold turkey's getting stale, tonight I'm eating crow / Fermented salmonella poison oak no" he is hell-bent on getting out of his tree. A funky, mostly bass backing that reminds the listener of the Kinks is the vehicle.

Grouch ★ ★

It's interesting that while Kerplunk!, Dookie and Insomniac attempted successfully at times to be rather profound and philosophical, with Nimrod the band tried to tone this approach down a little. 'The Grouch', for example, is a set of miserable whinings from a fictional old man with an attitude, such as: "I've decomposed, and my gut's getting fat / Oh my God I'm turning out like my dad / I'm always rude, I've got a bad attitude / The world owes me, so fuck you!"

Redundant ★ ★ ★ ★

'Redundant' became a Green Day hit thanks solely to the ingenious descending chorus, which ran "Now I cannot speak, I lost my voice / I'm speechless and redundant". Almost Beatles-like, with falsetto harmonies and a stop-start rhythm that alternates with the verses, it was a deserved classic and remains essential listening to this day.

Scattered ★ ★ ★

Cleverly, band and producer continued the harmonies trick through lines such as "Open the past and present / And the future too" in 'Scattered', which was similar to 'Redundant' in structure and sentiment. Were Green Day growing up so soon? It certainly seemed that way.

All The Time ★ ★ ★

Post-punk influences such as The Cars and Blondie would occasionally rear their heads in Armstrong's writing, and here's an early example, with Billie Joe's huge guitar sounds toned down to a minimal scrub and Dirnt's treble dialled up. It's another deft tale of frustration and running out of time, with the singer murmuring: "Promises, promises, it was all set in stone, cross my heart and hope to die".

Worry Rock ★ ★ ★

Another homage to the early sounds that had filled Green Day's ears as children, 'Worry Rock' contains a line "And I'll guarantee we'll have the road" which contains exactly the same melody as "Making all his nowhere plans for nobody" in the Beatles' 'Nowhere Man'. Is this a sign of early influences, or just a sly piss-take out of Green Day's fanbase? Either way, the song sounds great.

Platypus (I Hate You) ★ ★ ★

Sub-hardcore viciousness makes itself felt for the first time in 'Platypus', which contains a surprisingly graphic tirade of insults "Dickhead, fuck-face, cock-smoking, motherfucking, asshole, dirty twat, waste of semen, I hope you die!" and the more thought-out line "I'll stand above you just to piss on your grave". Who's the target of such ire? No-one knows.

Last Ride In ★ ★ ★

An ethereal, soundtrack-like guitar and keyboard workout, 'Last Ride In' evoked the eerie Twin Peaks-style ambience of Angelo Badalamenti and serves as a pause for breath halfway through this fairly intense album, which – as always with Green Day – was full of emotional rollercoasters. This was a mellow trough along the way…

Jinx ★ ★ ★

Ostensibly a simple punk anthem, 'Jinx' boasts slightly over-simple lines such as "Torture me, I've been a bad boy / Nail me to the cross until you have won", which seem to indicate that Green Day know what's expected of them and are just about still willing to play the game. But any song which includes the word 'nemesis' isn't just for frat-boys.

Haushinka ★ ★

"Haushinka is a girl with a peculiar name" sings Billie Joe, with sweet harmonies drenched over every line. He goes on to explain how he missed out on her love – through cowardice, ill-judgment or missed opportunity he does not say – but doesn't offer much more than this, leaving off at the end in simple frustration.

Walking Alone ★ ★ ★

"Sometimes I should just keep my mouth shut, or only say hello" grinds out Billie Joe over the tough, upbeat, uptempo punk that Green Day do so well. Once again he's celebrating his faults, with particular attention paid to the fact that he's alone and perhaps unloved too. Was ever a songwriter born who made so much of his failings, and those of his contemporaries, but who also wrote songs of tenderness and passion?

Reject ★ ★

"I'll see you in hell, so when the smoke clears here I am, your reject all-American," promises Armstrong in another fast song – not much different from any other Green Day composition of the era, other than it plumbs depths of introspection with a degree of obscurity that other songs have so far failed to match.

Take Back ★ ★ ★

With 'Take Back' Green Day get into fighting territory once again, this time with genuine violence spewing out of Armstrong's mouth. He swears, "You pushed me once too far again / I'd like to break your fucking teeth / Stick a knife in the centre of your back / You better grow some eyes in the back of your head" – not much doubt about his intentions there, then. The backing is furious, hardcore and unrelenting. Perhaps this song is best viewed as the antithesis of 'Good Riddance', coming up soon?

King For A Day ★ ★

A comedy song with burlesque horns and lyrics about cross-dressing ("My daddy threw me in therapy / He thinks I'm not a real man / Who put the drag in the drag queen / Don't knock it until you've tried it…"), 'King For A Day' is best viewed as a bit of harmless filler between the angey songs on this album and what came next.

Good Riddance (Time Of Your Life) ★ ★ ★ ★ ★

A vile stain on the bedsheet of pop-punk or a glorious flowering of songwriting and arranging talent that surpassed its creators to become a deserved mega-hit? It's your decision, but I'll take the latter – no matter that the Wal-Mart generation bought into

Green Day when they'd never even heard of 'Basket Case'. True talent will out, no matter what the environment, and 'Time Of Your Life', with its heart-rending strings, was a genuine musical landmark.

Prosthetic Head ★ ★ ★
After the surprisingly effective aesthetics of 'Good Riddance' comes a snarled, possibly anti-military diatribe in the form of 'Prosthetic Head', which begins "I see you, down in the front line / Such a sight for sore eyes, you're a suicide makeover". The sliding guitar riff and the sneers that follow it are a reminder, perhaps, that Green Day are punk to their core and that 'Good Riddance' would have been too cheesy if it had been left on the end of Insomniac like a grand finale.

Conclusion
Insomniac works on most levels – sonically, lyrically and musically – but was inevitably hampered by having to follow in the footsteps of Dookie, one of the biggest-selling albums ever. It's by turns clever, stupid, knowing and complaining, suiting both creators and its target listenership with all those criteria. More, and better, was to come.

Overall rating: ★ ★ ★

HITCHIN' A RIDE
(Single, 11 October 1997)

Tracklisting: Hitchin' A Ride / Sick Of Me / Espionage

Perhaps not the obvious choice of lead-off single from Insomniac, but 'Hitchin' A Ride' did the job of reminding people how angry Green Day could be before the enomous impact of the super-sweet and sugary 'Good Riddance' single three months later…

Overall rating: ★ ★ ★

GOOD RIDDANCE (TIME OF YOUR LIFE)
(Single, 31 January 1998)

Tracklisting: Good Riddance (Time Of Your Life) / Suffocate / You Lied / Rotting

Typically, Green Day matched 'Time Of Your Life' up with some snotty, aggressive punk tunes on the single so that people wouldn't think they were wusses (Metallica did the same thing with 'Nothing Else Matters' and the Chili Peppers with 'Soul To Squeeze') but they had no need to worry. By the time the song smashed into the charts, everybody knew who Green Day were.

Overall rating: ★ ★ ★ ★ ★

REDUNDANT
(Single, 9 May 1998)

Tracklisting: Redundant / The Grouch (Live) / Paper Lanterns (Live)

A final kiss-off from the Nimrod campaign to sign off this stage of Green Day's career, the 'Redundant' single was the last real release to play the 'I'm a dumb young punk teen with no future' card. After this, Green Day were just too rich, too old and too sophisticated to play that particular trick convincingly: and anyway, they had other fish to fry.

Overall rating: ★ ★ ★

MINORITY
(Single, 30 September 2000)

Tracklisting: Minority / Brat (Live From Prague) / 86 (Live From Tokyo)

Pleasant as 'Minority' is, it's obvious why Green Day chose 'Brat' and '86' – among the most aggressive songs they've recorded – to pair it with for the single, especially as those songs linked well with the previous albums. Remember, in autumn 2000 they'd had almost a year and a half away from the charts – they needed something memorable to kickstart their return with.

Overall rating: ★ ★ ★

WARNING
(Album, 14 October 2000)

Tracklisting: Warning / Blood, Sex And Booze / Church On Sunday / Fashion Victim / Castaway / Misery / Deadbeat Holiday / Hold On / Jackass / Waiting / Minority / Macy's Day Parade

Warning ★ ★ ★ ★
The catchiest intro to any Green Day album ever, apart from American Idiot of course, 'Warning' stands tall on its ludicrously hummable chorus of "Warning, live without warning" and the ascending/descending lick that follows it. The rest of the song, a pleasant, mostly acoustic-sounding strum, is hardly the aggressive Green Day of before – a brave move for a new album.

Blood, Sex And Booze ★ ★ ★
Another domination and torture song – but this time ambling and pleasant rather than wide-eyed and speedy – 'Blood, Sex And Booze' is Billie Joe's tale of humiliation and punishment, all told with a cheery smile. "Thank you sir, strike up another mandolin of discipline / Throw me to the dogs / Let them eat my flesh down / To the wood" he mumbles, almost apologetically. Weird, but interesting.

Church On Sunday ★ ★ ★

Based on a simple rock'n'roll chord sequence but boosted by the knowing themes of compromise and blackmail ("If I promise to go to church on Sunday / Will you go with me on Friday night?"), 'Church On Sunday' would have made a decent single, had Warners been thinking straight (and perhaps not been afraid of offending the American moral majority).

Fashion Victim ★ ★

Ripping into the media, the fashion industry and its followers with equal abandon, 'Fashion Victim' sees Billie Joe mocking celebrity ailments with his usual attractively black humour ("So when you're dancing through your wardrobe / Do the anorex-a-go-go") with a highly melodic vocal line. As Green Day slowly became icons, so they were beginning to revile their environment, it seems.

Castaway ★

Veering dangerously close to the kind of comedy nu-rock that was being played by frat-boy acts such as New Found Glory and Alien Ant Farm, 'Castaway' is the story of a man who leaves it all behind to start again on his own ("I'm on a mission / In the destination unknown"). The vocal effects and lightweight music don't do the song any favours, though, and the sentiments are fluffy.

Misery ★

The most insignificant song on this album, 'Misery' is an oblique story of characters who fall into misfortune over a hardly-realised backing. Lines like "Mr. Whirly had a catastrophic incident / He fell into the city by the bay" don't lend it much depth, unfortunately.

Deadbeat Holiday ★ ★

I challenge anyone not to hum the title line of this little ditty, even if the song does lack weight and comes with glum lines such as "Last chance to piss it all away / Nothing but hell to pay / When the lights are going down". The song, and the album in general, seems to belong to Mike Dirnt's bass – which, while a fine thing, leaves the songs feeling a little flavourless.

Hold On ★ ★ ★

The loping rhythm, limp guitars and cheerful vocals on songs such as 'Hold On' and its immediate predecessors may make Warning slightly difficult to stomach – but it has to be admitted that when Green Day do black humour mixed with positivity, they do it well. As Billie Joe urges, when "Nothing's left to cling onto / You got to hold on / Hold on to yourself…"

Jackass ★ ★

"I don't care if I don't care / No-one ever said that life is fair," laughs Armstrong, before adding that while everyone loves a joke, no-one likes a fool. But who's the fool? We're not told…

Waiting ★ ★ ★

Evoking the spirit of the Kinks and maybe even the Small Faces on this slight bit of pop, 'Waiting' threw excellent melodies all over the place and even used a descending chord sequence on the line "I'm so much closer than I have ever known...". Genius, if also rather cheap – Green Day have done far better elsewhere.

Minority ★ ★ ★

A trademark bit of pop-rock that bears little resemblance to anything punkish, 'Minority' was the best that Warning had to offer in the way of a single. It works well thanks to its yobbish but cool chorus of "Down with the moral majority / 'Cause I want to be the minority", a mockery of those who deliberately side with the underdog.

Macy's Day Parade ★ ★ ★

A considered, strolling and pensive ending to Warning, 'Macy's

Day Parade' sees Armstrong ponder big questions such as life, happiness and "economy sized dreams of hope". After warbling "When I was a kid I thought / I wanted all the things that I haven't got" against a slight, loping background of clean guitar, he brings this elegant but obscure album to a close.

Conclusion

Neither as accessible as Dookie nor as experimental as Nimrod, Warning is chock full of pop melodies and pleasant tunes, and it's obvious that the band – and Billie Joe in particular – are on their way to another place, musically. The lyrics are deeper than before, with less attention paid to the endless self-examination that made certain songs a little wearing on earlier albums, too. Unfortunately, it all feels rather slight and unfocused, with the rage of earlier albums nowhere to be seen.

Overall rating: ★ ★

WARNING
(Single, 23 December 2000)

Tracklisting: Warning / Scumbag / I Don't Want To Know If You're Lonely

The best song on Warning by far, the title track single was a deserved rejuvenation for Green Day as the new millennium got underway. Many fans who had dismissed them in the era of nu-metal regained some respect in its wake.

Overall rating: ★ ★ ★ ★

WAITING
(Single, 10 November 2001)

Tracklisting: Waiting / She (Live) / F.O.D. (Live)

The concept of pairing the rather nice and inoffensive 'Waiting' with two live burnouts of vintage Green Day tracks paid off, although as the age of downloading took off the importance of single tracklistings began to diminish markedly.

Overall rating: ★ ★ ★

INTERNATIONAL SUPERHITS

(Album and DVD, 24 November 2001)

Tracklisting: Maria / Poprocks & Coke / Longview / Welcome To Paradise / Basket Case / When I Come Around / She / J.A.R. / Geek Stink Breath / Jaded / Walking Contradiction / Stuck With Me / Hitchin' A Ride / Time Of Your Life (Good Riddance) / Redundant / Nice Guys Finish Last / Minority / Warning / Waiting / Macy's Day Parade

Maria ★ ★ ★ ★

A superior bit of pop-punk from the much-evolved band, 'Maria' had to be a decent effort if it was to incentivise the buyer to invest in International Superhits – and so it was. Referencing the political issues of the day in vaguely seditious terms ("Bring in the head of the government / The dog ate the document / Somebody shot the President / And no-one knows where Maria went?"), 'Maria' made Green Day sound switched on.

Poprocks And Coke ★ ★

An optimistic, if not especially memorable, cleanly-strummed jaunt through some cheerful "I'll be there" lyrics, 'Poprocks And Coke" is as fizzy and unthreatening as its title. Why it was chosen to promote the album is a mystery.

For other tracks on International Superhits see parent albums.

Conclusion

A Green Day greatest hits compilation – and why not? They'd served their time by 2001 – almost a decade of hard slog, by God – and this nifty little collection served to remind the 15-year-old fans who were, uh, five when they'd started out, what a useful history lay behind them. A kid could have compiled it (or Tre Cool, a-huh-a-huh-a-huh), so obvious were the career highlights, but having them all in one place at least saved you the trouble of logging on to Soulseek, eh? The two bonus tracks were fine, if no real reason to buy.

Overall rating: ★ ★ ★

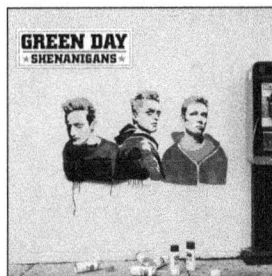

POPROCKS AND COKE
(Single, 1 January 2001)

Tracklisting: Poprocks And Coke / She (Live) / F.O.D. (Live)

While 'Poprocks And Coke' didn't do anything that you couldn't hear on any of a dozen other Green Day songs, at least it didn't outstay its welcome. The live bonus tracks were amusing and welcome.

Overall rating: ★ ★ ★

SHENANIGANS
(Album, 13 July 2002)

Tracklisting: Suffocate / Desensitized / You Lied / Outsider / Don't Wanna Fall In Love / Espionage / I Want To Be On TV / Scumbag / Tired Of Waiting For You / Sick Of Me / Rotting / Do Da Do / On The Wagon / Ha Ha You're Dead

Suffocate ★ ★ ★

"Three a.m., I'm drunk again / My head is standing underneath my puke" starts Armstrong with this dismal tale of intoxicated misery. Whoever the central character is, he's not happy, although this exquisitely harmonised song is solidly enjoyable.

Desensitized ★ ★ ★ ★

Too good for B-side status, 'Desensitized' is a melodic, layered song that references the usual Armstrong fears ("I wanna watch the bomb / Blow the masses high") in a highly listenable manner.

You Lied ★ ★

A stamping, staccato, almost Marilyn Manson-esque glam-rock snarl, 'You Lied' refers to Pinocchio piercing tongues and is moderately interesting. But essential? No.

Outsider ★ ★

Predictable punk by numbers, 'Outsider' doesn't offer an awful lot other than the repeated claim of "Oh I'm an outsider outside of everything". It's upbeat, I suppose, but that's not really enough, is it?

Don't Wanna Fall In Love ★ ★

Hillbilly rock with a silly polka beat from Tre, a corny guitar solo and lyrics such as "Stay the fuck away from me because I don't believe in you, and I wanna sit here all my life alone"? Highly entertaining!

Espionage ★ ★

This gritty song straight from the dark heart – well, perhaps not all that dark – of Green Day. It's frothy, fast and light, just like an espresso latte, and about as durable.

I Want To Be On TV ★ ★ ★ ★

A fun, disposable way of spending three minutes, 'I Want To Be On TV' is frat-rock personified – fast, stupid and catchy.

Armstrong, in full yobbo mode, yells "Gonna have some free cocaine / Wanna wear my Calvin Kleins / Then the world will be all mine". Classic stuff.

Scumbag ★ ★ ★ ★

"Have you ever stopped to think before you opened up your mouth? / Because every time you do, it's the same thing again and again" sneers Armstrong. A pacey, energetic tune with balls, 'Scumbag' is where Shenanigans truly excels.

Tired Of Waiting For You ★ ★ ★ ★

A superb cover of the Kinks classic, 'Tired...' replicates the laconic vocals and strolling rhythm of the original without – as Green Day must surely have been tempted to do – amping it up into a punk anthem.

Sick Of Me ★ ★ ★

With its repeated line of 'sick of me', harmonised in such a way that it burrows into the listener's brain and refuses to move, this song might well have been Green Day laughing at their fanbase. Nevertheless, it works.

Rotting ★ ★

"Thorns shred my fingertips / And drip toxic blood..." drawls Armstrong in this mock-Gothic deathbed ballad. The punk Sisters Of Mercy?

Do Da Da ★

A depressive, droning song that will have most listeners leaping for the skip button, 'Do Da Da' has little to recommend it.

On The Wagon ★ ★ ★

Pure pop – and that is meant as a compliment – 'On The Wagon' is a lazy shuffle through a drunk person's apologies, and quite a nice way of exiting the record...

Ha Ha You're Dead ★ ★

High-quality malevolence ("When your ship is going down / I'll go out and paint the town") never sounded so good, especially when juxtaposed against a mellow rock backing.

Conclusion

It seems to most sane observers that Shenanigans was a mere gap-filler, a way of gathering the single B-sides and other limited-edition ephemera that Green Day had recorded across the years – without actually offering much to the hardcore fan. The result is just that: lightweight, even if some of its content is rather good. It remains the Green Day you least need to have.

Overall rating: ★ ★

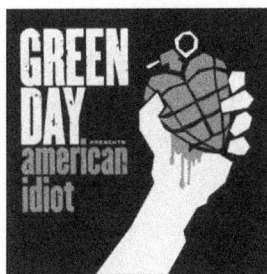

AMERICAN IDIOT
(Album, 21 September 2004)

Tracklisting: American Idiot / Jesus Of Suburbia / City Of The Damned / I Don't Care / Dearly Beloved / Tales Of Another Broken Home / Holiday / Boulevard Of Broken Dreams / Are We Waiting / St. Jimmy / Give Me Novacaine / She's A Rebel / Extraordinary Girl / Letterbomb / Wake Me Up When September Ends / The Death Of St. Jimmy / East 12th St. / Nobody Likes You / Rock & Roll Girlfriend / Were Coming Home Again / Whatsername

American Idiot ★ ★ ★ ★

It's mainstream, it's clinically produced and it was a global hit, of course, so it's easy to hate 'American Idiot' – but don't. It's a masterpiece of a song, clutching the listener by the earlobes and refusing to let go until that top-line melody ("Don't wanna be...") had insinuated itself into your brain and made itself comfortably at home. Oh, and that massive riff made 'American

Idiot' the first convincing case for Green Day to be reclassified as a metal band.

Jesus Of Suburbia ★ ★ ★
1 Jesus Of Suburbia
2 City Of The Damned
3 I Don't Care
4 Dearly Beloved
5 Tales Of Another Broken Home

The first of two suites that American Idiot offers is expansive and lyrical, with Armstrong variously mentioning that "No-one ever died for my sins in hell / As far as I can tell" and extending the concept through religious imagery with panache. Righteous.

Holiday ★ ★ ★ ★
With its beautiful cascades of chords and harmony vocals, 'Holiday' invokes every Bush-era image going ("Can I get another Amen? (Amen!) / There's a flag wrapped around a score of men (Hey!) / A gag, a plastic bag on a monument" with dazzling vigour.

Boulevard Of Broken Dreams ★ ★ ★ ★
Damn, the hits just kept coming – what was Billie Joe Armstrong eating? A slow, near-perfect stroll through massively reverbed vocals, an achingly beautiful repeated guitar motif and Dirnt's crystal-clear bass anchoring it all, 'Boulevard...' seemed at once to be the sound of Green Day hitting their maturity and remembering where it all started.

Are We The Waiting ★ ★ ★ ★
Another gorgeous ballad – was Armstrong feeling almost too relaxed? – 'Are We The Waiting?' sounds exactly like the images it evokes ("Starry nights, city lights coming down over me / Skyscrapers and stargazers in my head") – all expanses of light and shade.

St. Jimmy ★ ★ ★

The big concept tune introducing St. Jimmy – whose spectral presence informs the whole album – is furious, upbeat and pure Green Day: as he says, "I am the son of a bitch and Edgar Allen Poe!"

Give Me Novacaine ★ ★

A love song to anaesthesia, 'Give Me…' is exactly what you'd expect – a spacious, open tale of blankness and escape.

She's A Rebel ★ ★

As with 'Maria', Armstrong sings here of a 'dangerous' female with hidden intentions, over a raucous but forgettable backing.

Extraordinary Girl ★ ★

This mellow song – of "an ordinary girl in an extraordinary world" – is more filler, even if it has a certain charm of its own.

Letterbomb ★ ★ ★

"Where have all the bastards gone?" asks Billie Joe in a blizzard of riffage – like the title track, a song with balls.

Wake Me Up When September Ends ★ ★ ★ ★

A rock anthem – that dreaded phrase – that was slow and majestic enough to require a lighters-aloft moment when performed live, but was also heavy enough for the moshpit, 'Wake Me Up When September Ends' was almost the perfect song. Not that anybody really cared about the lyrics, conceptually honed though they were: it was the simple, descending chorus line that hooked everybody in. Another reason to invest in rock's premier idiot millionaires.

Homecoming ★ ★ ★ ★
1 The Death Of St. Jimmy
2 East 12th St.
3 Nobody Likes You

4 Rock And Roll Girlfriend

5 We're Coming Home Again

The second concept suite on Idiot is ambitious, like the first, but appealing: the band ascend peaks of anger before sinking back into melancholy, lending the album huge variation. There's much here for anyone, fan or not…

Whatsername ★ ★

"I remember the face but I can't recall the name / Now I wonder how whatsername has been" chuckles the singer. The song, too, isn't memorable.

Conclusion

If not the best album Green Day have ever made, American Idiot is probably the one they'll be most remembered for – by under-30s, at least. Older listeners will always come back to Dookie. But the sounds, the lyrics and the anger of the album gain it an excellent rating.

Overall rating: ★ ★ ★ ★

AMERICAN IDIOT
(Single, 31 August 2004)

Tracklisting: American Idiot / Governator / Shoplifter

You can't really argue with this single, although Green Day might have felt a touch of pre-release nerves when wondering if the masses would buy into their sanitised anti-Bush crusade. The song is just too gripping not to have been a major hit, especially as the rock scene was in slightly feeble shape at that point in 2004. The B-sides were worth investigating, especially the tongue-in-Arnie's-cheek 'Governator'.

Overall rating: ★ ★ ★ ★

BOULEVARD OF BROKEN DREAMS
(Single, 25 January 2004)

Tracklisting: Boulevard Of Broken Dreams / Letterbomb (Recorded on September 21st 2004 at Irving Plaza, New York) / American Idiot (Live) / She's A Rebel (Live)

More of an encapsulation of the American Idiot phenomenon than a single release on its own merits, 'Boulevard Of Broken Dreams' – with its three live tracks – sums up something of the hysteria surrounding Green Day in late 2004 and early 2005. It's a stirring song in its own right, and comes into its own here.

Overall rating: ★ ★ ★ ★

BULLET IN A BIBLE
(Album and DVD, 15 November 2005)

Tracklisting: American Idiot / Jesus Of Suburbia / Holiday / Are We The Waiting / St. Jimmy / Longview / Hitchin A Ride / Brain Stew / Jaded / Knowledge / Basket Case / She / King For A Day / Shout / Wake Me Up When September Ends / Minority / Maria / Boulevard Of Broken Dreams / We Are The Champions / Time Of Your Life (Good Riddance)

Bullet In A Bible would never have been released without the massive success of American Idiot, of course, but it still stands up on its own merits as a decent document of the lavish show that Green Day put on for the adoring masses after a decade in the spotlight. It's a long way from the Gilman Street days, but the album and DVD work perfectly as a document of that very journey.

Overall rating: ★ ★ ★ ★

FOR THEIR NEXT RELEASE, *WARNING*, *GREEN DAY* TONED DOWN THE AGGRESSION. HOWEVER, THEY WERE NOT *TONE-DEAF*. FOR THE FIRST TIME, THEY RECORDED AND MIXED THE MUSIC THEMSELVES. *WARNING* HIT THE RACKS FALL OF 2000.

IN SUPPORT OF *GREATEST HITS* AND B-SIDE RELEASES, *GREEN DAY* TOURED MORE AND DUBBED THEIR JOURNEY THE *POP DISASTER TOUR*. FOR SOME, IT MAY HAVE BEEN A DISASTER TO HAVE SECOND-RATE PUNKS, *BLINK 182*, FOLLOW INFLUENTIAL PUNK-ELDERS, *GREEN DAY* ON STAGE.
EITHER WAY, *THE BANDS* PLAYED ON.

IN THE FALL OF 2004, *GREEN DAY* DROPPED ALL INHIBITIONS AND CREATED A *POLITICAL* MASTERPIECE IN THE SHAPE OF A ROCK OPERA CALLED *AMERICAN IDIOT*. THE ALBUM BLEW MOST ROCK N ROLL STANDARDS *OUT OF THE WATER* AND PLACED *GREEN DAY* BACK ON TOP.
HOW WILL THEY FOLLOW THAT? WE'LL LET YOU KNOW *WHEN* IT HAPPENS.

C.ROAD

116

INTERVIEW WITH
LARRY LIVERMORE

Green Day are still, twenty years after their inception, one of the biggest names in rock music today. This book offers interviews with two of the key players in the band's history, both past and present, Larry Livermore and John Lucasey, as well as a short talk with Ben Myers, a leading Green Day authority.

Green Day seemingly appeared out of nowhere with their 1994 album Dookie, a hugely successful album that catapulted Billie-Joe Armstrong, Mike Dirnt and Tré Cool to international superstardom. In fact, two of the youthful trio had begun making music some seven years earlier, under the name Sweet Children. Lookout records, founded by Larry Livermore, were the first record company to spot the band's potential. In this recent interview, Livermore tells the story of the band's early years in his own words.

Q Why did you start a label?
Well, the quick answer is that at the time I didn't like any of the music that was on the radio or in the shops, and so I reckoned that if I ever wanted to have any records that I wanted to listen to, I'd have to make them myself. That's the simplest way I can explain it. It evolved from a little magazine I was doing at the time. I was living way up in the rural mountain area of northern California, and I'd started doing this little magazine to amuse myself and express myself, and I'd had a bad encounter with some of the neighbours. There were a lot of pot growers, a lot of marijuana growers around the area and they didn't like the fact that I was writing about that. They actually came 'round to my house in a delegation and threatened to burn my house down

if I didn't stop writing about the area. I said that since I wanted to keep my house, I would write about other things, so I started to write about music, specifically punk rock. That led into me starting a band, and when the band had been playing for about a year, I thought, 'Well, I know how to make a fanzine. How much harder can it be to put out records?' So I put out a record by my band, and although I didn't realise it at the time, that was the beginning of the label.

Q Cool, great, thank you. Where do Green Day come into it all? Were they already on the scene?
Oh no, all of this happened before Green Day even existed. In fact, the connection to Green Day is that my band needed a drummer, and the closest thing I could find to a drummer was this crazy kid that lived about a mile down the road. He was 12 at the time, and he'd never played drums in his life, but he was a big show off. He had a big mouth and I guess what you'd call charisma. Somehow I got it into my head that, 'Well, he might be a good drummer,' and I asked him to come over and try his hand at the drums. He wasn't half bad. He had enthusiasm and he could keep a beat, so it turned out well. His nickname was Tré, because he was the third in his family with the same name. So I said to him, 'Well, you need a punk rock name now,' and we settled on Tré Cool. As we know, a few years later he was drumming for Green Day. But for the first five years of his punk rock career he was playing in my band, The Lookouts. So I guess that was the beginning of the connection.

Q So was this all happening up in the mountains? Where did you gig?
Our first gig was in a car park down on the side of the highway, with 18-wheelers rolling by and dust blowing all over the place. The audience were maybe 30 or 40 local hippies, parents of the other kids in the band, and curious neighbours; that was about

it. It was also a kind of a ritual up there in the mountains to have big parties every few weeks at somebody's house, because it was so far to town that there wasn't a whole lot else going on. So you had these frontier parties that reminded me of the old barn raisings you see in movies; we played at a couple of those. That didn't go over too well, but the people up there were fairly tolerant because music was in short supply. Entertainment of any sort was in short supply! Then later on, we started playing in town - well, 'town' is a big word for it. It was really a collection of gas stations, two bars and a store. We didn't go over too well there either; we got chased off the stage, and I was punched out on one occasion. We didn't start playing down in San Francisco or Berkley or Oakland until a year or so after we'd formed. That just came about because I'd been going down there for shows (it was almost 200 miles away, but I'd go down for punk rock gigs occasionally, because it was the only place you could find them at the time), and by talking to people I ended up getting the band invited to play at one of them. From then on, we'd go down to the bay area about once a month. I wouldn't say that

we got a great reception, but we got a better reception than we'd been getting up in the mountains. So that's how we came to be associated with the bay area scene.

Q How did you meet the other guys from Green Day?
Well, you need to remember that Green Day had a different drummer for the first two years of their existence, and he was somebody I already knew from the punk scene. This was 1988, and by that time my label had taken off; we'd had maybe five or ten releases. One of them was of a local band called Isocracy, and their drummer was a real character. He'd phoned me up way back in '86 when he was still in high school, and asked me how to get gigs and how this whole punk thing happened. I'd invited him to play at one of our shows, and within a year his band had taken over the scene. Their big routine wasn't so much musical; they would collect all of the rubbish on their way to the gig and then throw it at the audience, and the audience would throw it back at them. The drummer's name was John Kiffmyer, but he went by the name of Al Sabronte. He had taken the name from the suburb where he grew up, El Sabronte, which means 'the leftover' in Spanish. Anyway, I'd been hanging out with him for about a year when his band Isocracy had broken up. He phoned me and said, 'Hey, I got a new band and we're called Sweet Children. These two 16-year-old kids are playing in it with me, and they're really great. Is there any place we could play?' There wasn't much going on at the time, but Tré (who, at that point, was still our drummer in the Lookouts) was organising some stupid party for a bunch of his high school mates on the Friday night. I said, 'You're welcome to come and play, but there's no money. It's a 140 mile drive, winter is setting in, and I don't even know if anybody will turn up,' and he said, 'Well, we'll be there!' And sure enough, they drove over that snowy road in the mountains and turned up at the party. That was the first night I met Billie and Mike. I guess it

must have been October/November of 1988. You want the rest of the story?

Q Yeah. Who drove them, by the way?
That was Al; he did all the driving and all the arranging of the shows at that time. He was about two years older than they were. At the time, they were only 16, so Al was the den mother. I don't know if you know that expression in England, it comes from the cub scouts.. In any case, the boys were brilliant at playing and writing songs, as well as performing. But as you would expect from a couple of 16-year-olds, they couldn't do a lot else for themselves, and so Al pretty much arranged everything; told them to get in the band wagon bus and drove. So they turned up all ready to play. But it turned out that because the weather so bad and because it was so far into the mountains from town (it was a different mountain from where we lived, but it was still 20 miles from town), none of the area kids had bothered coming to the party, so the audience was only about five strong. Billie and Mike didn't express disappointment or disillusionment at all. They just came in and got on with it. First, we had to set up a generator because there was no electricity, and then we had to start a fire in the wood stove because it was freezing cold. Finally, we lit a lot of candles to illuminate the stage, and then they played. I still think it must have been one of the best shows of their lives. Of course, they've played many sensational shows since then, but I've always said it was like the Beatles at Shea stadium. I mean, they played to these five curious kids who'd never seen a punk band before, and they played their hearts out. Billie had that perfect combination of arrogance and humility that marked him out as a star; even then at 16. He just sang right to every one of those kids and thanked them for coming and asked them if they were enjoying the show. Near the end of their set, a couple of the kids had to get up and leave, because

they had a curfew. They apologised, and Billy thanked them again for coming and got on with the rest of the show. This was probably only the third or fourth show that Sweet Children had ever played, and yet, before it was even half over, I was saying in my head, 'I've got to do a record with these guys, I don't know if anybody will buy it, but people have to know about this music. It has to be immortalised.' When they had finished playing, Billie came up to me and asked shyly, 'What did you think? Did you like what we're doing?' And I just said, 'Well, I'd love to do a record with you guys.' He looked a little bit taken aback, but he just said, 'Oh, okay man,' and that was that.

Q Why do you think they had so much fire in their bellies? I mean, some kids have and some kids haven't...
What motivated Green Day was Billie and Mike specifically. I'm not a psychologist, and I think that a fair bit has already been written and discussed on that subject. But because of their family backgrounds, they were probably driven in a way that a lot of kids with easier, ordinary lives weren't. I don't know if I'm even qualified to go into it, but I interviewed Billie a few years ago for a magazine article and he told me about his father being a musician and his mother working really, really hard to survive after his father died. It's just something that really drove him to do something with his life, but at the same time he didn't really have a whole lot of other skills beside musical ones. He told me many times, 'I don't know what I would do or could do if I didn't play music.' Mike had had a similarly rough life. I don't know if it's my place to go into detail about it, it's been spoken about in lots of other places, but I know that they met each other at a very young age - I think it was around ten or eleven, something like that - and they'd been jamming in their backyard all those years since. I think that they'd had several incarnations of the band; the only name I can remember offhand is Blood Rage, which was a metal thing that they did. None of

it really got them anywhere, but obviously all that time they were learning to play together and to write together, so by the time they met up with Al, it was just waiting to happen. That was their missing ingredient. Al not only had the organisational abilities, but also the connections and inspirations to say, 'Hey, we don't need to sit here rehearsing and making all these demos, there's already a punk scene. We can just go and play. They'll love it!" And I think that just set them free. It was so exciting to be that age and all of a sudden have hundreds of kids out there, appreciating your music. I can only imagine what it would've been like for me to be playing in a cool band at that age. So that, on top of their undeniable talent and dedication, kick-started them and sent them into orbit.

Q I went to their town [Rodeo, California], and there was just nothing happening; there was nobody on the street and it was so oppressive. You can see why they'd want to do something about their situation.
Yeah. It's a typical American blue-collar suburb, very similar to the place I grew up, outside of Detroit, so I recognised the feeling right away. It's part of what made it so exciting to work with bands like them, because it was a chance to revisit my own teenage-hood. I'd been lucky to see something like that happen in Detroit when I was a teenager. The Motown scene started when I was about 14, and although I wasn't part of it, it was close-by. I was able to see that they were a bunch of people from the working class, from the under-class and from the housing projects. These people were turning America on its ear by creating this whole new sound, this whole new culture. That was something that always really inspired me. So when I saw this new sound coming out of the East Bay working class suburbs, I knew I wanted to be a part of it.

There was no definite plan at that point, because as I said, it was only their third or fourth show. I mentioned it to my business partner [David Hayes], and he was dubious, with good reason; they were a bit poppier than the bands we were use to (I'd compared them to the Beatles), but the kind of records that we'd put out so far were definitely punk records. I had the feeling that a lot of the punks we normally sold to probably wouldn't like them that much, and that they wouldn't sell that much. But I still thought that it was worthwhile to make a record, and my partner begrudgingly accepted! The EP was recorded the following January, and it was scheduled to come out in April. About two weeks before the release date, we still had no record cover, no name, or anything else. We had the records ready to be pressed, and the band came to me and said, 'Oh, we've changed our name. We don't want to be Sweet Children anymore.' I just blew a gasket and said, 'You can't do that, that's ridiculous! You're not that well known as it is, and the handful of people that are going to buy your record are looking for a record by Sweet Children! What are you going to call yourself now?' They said, 'We're gonna be Green Day.' I said, 'that doesn't even make any sense, that's a stupid name,' and they said 'Well, it makes sense to us.' I didn't have that many arguments with them over the years I worked with them, but it was probably because I learnt from that one that it was pointless. Once they'd decided what was going to happen, that's what happened. I could rant and rave all day if I wanted to and they would just look off into the distance. Eventually, after I'd said my piece they'd say, 'Yeah, but this is what we want to do.' So, we scraped together some…well, I guess you'd call it artwork. My partner, David Hayes, made up a logo (It was a pretty cool one that you still see sometimes today.) and he basically made a Xerox sheet on green paper to go with their new name, and rushed these records out. They didn't sell very well at first. At that time, Green Day were still having trouble getting gigs at Gilman Street [the club in

Berkley, California that was the focus for the scene at the time] because some of the more hardcore punks there would say that they weren't really punk. The band persisted, though, and when they couldn't play at Gilman they'd play other places. Over the following year, the record got a little bit of a buzz. Some people slagged it off for being too poppy, but others said, 'Hey, it's really catchy.' So we sold about 1000 copies, which wasn't great, but wasn't bad for a 7" at that time. In terms of music I thought that it was brilliant, and almost exactly a year later we did an album.

Q Do you think that the scene held them back in any way?
I think that it did, for both of them. It did hold them back in some ways, but on the other hand, I don't think it would have been possible for them to do what they did without that scene. I mean, Gilman Street was a convergence of several scenes - the punk scene has always had factions; you've got the crusties and the hardcores, and nowadays, the emos and the pop-punkers - and for most of the time they'd barely even speak to each other, but at Gilman Street they'd all come together in a common enterprise and agree to tolerate each other for a greater purpose. There was an uneasy truce between these people, and it made this really cool grass-roots scene possible. Before Gilman, there weren't a lot of places to play. A venue would open up only to close down a few weeks later because there'd been a fight or a spate of vandalism. In that sense, Gilman made everything possible for Green Day, and it also created a market that we were able to sell our records to. Also, I think that there was just enough resistance, just enough teasing and heckling from the more snotty punks, to inspire Green Day to try a bit harder and push on a bit more. No, I don't really think it was really down to me to encourage them, I think that they were not a band that needed encouragement because they were really self-motivated. It might have been another year or two before they

got a record out if it wasn't for me, but I'm sure that they would have eventually.

Q What were the first recording sessions like?
All I know really is what David told me: they came in, played their songs and were out of there really quickly. They very rarely had to do anything more than once. They were a record producer's dream because they knew all of their stuff perfectly and they didn't have to do re-takes. It was very cheap to do, and they produced some really great sounds, and some great songs.

Q Yeah, I wonder why you weren't there - maybe you trusted them...
Oh I did that. I trusted most of my bands. I thought that if a band was good enough to make a record, then they didn't need a babysitter in the studio. We also had a couple of producer/engineers that we worked with at the time who I trusted implicitly; one was Kevin Army, and the other was Andy Ernst who did all the early Green Day stuff. I knew he knew way more about it than I did, and if I sent a band to him, I knew that he would do a good job and wouldn't waste time or money. Some bands really wanted me to be there to hold their hands and encourage them, and some bands wanted me nowhere near the studio, and I was fine either way.

Q What happened to Al?
Al played on the first EP, the first album, and actually on the second EP which came out the summer after the first album in 1990; as I said earlier, he was invaluable to the band. I think he often gets overlooked now. I saw this article in Rolling Stone last summer, and Al didn't even get a mention. I'm pretty sure that the band would not have got through those first years without him, but the thing is, there was a socio-economic and cultural divide between Al, and Billie and Mike. Al had other

ambitions, other ideas. I put it down to them being blue-collar working class, and Al being more middles class, and from a more prosperous background. He had this idea that he wanted to go to college, and not just go to college but have the full-on university experience, living there and becoming part of it. So at the end of the summer of 1990, after they'd done their first tour and were really starting to get some recognition, he told Billie and Mike, 'I'm going to go away to university for two years to have this university experience,' and, as he put it, 'so we're going to have to put the band on hold for two years.; Billie and Mike were devastated. Billie was just 18 at the time and had just left school. He later told me that his whole life revolved around this band and he couldn't even comprehend what Al was on about. At the same time, he had had this romantic idea that the band doesn't just break up - you don't just have somebody quit and replace him - it's like a gang and you just stick together until the bitter end. So Billie thought it was over and he was heartbroken. Al went off to university up north and nothing happened for a couple of months. Around that time, The Lookouts had become increasingly inactive. We were all scattered around the country as well, so we had played our last show in July of 1990. Billie had come in to play with us. He played lead guitar and sang back-up vocals on our last recordings, and I guess that would have been the first time that Billy and Tré had played together. Later that autumn, Tré moved down to the Bay area to attend college, and he and Billie eventually ran into each other. I'd guess that one of them proposed that they try jamming together. The next thing I knew, Tré was going to play a show with Green Day as their fill-in drummer. It was almost like seeing Green Day for the first time again, because they had a whole new dimension. By this time, Tré had become a really excellent drummer. I knew that he was exactly what they needed and that he was going to be a great part of the band. Of course, I was sad at the same time, because I knew it would probably mean the end of The Lookouts. But I also knew that it would mean that Green Day were going to carry on and be even greater.

I think it was a bit of an awkward parting at first, because Al still had it in his mind that he was going to come back and play with the band when it was possible, during university vacations and holidays and all, and that Tré was only a fill-in drummer. In fact, a couple of times he did turn up at shows at the last minute and say, 'Oh, I'm here, we don't need you Tré,; and of course that was pretty upsetting for Tré, and for the band as a whole. Billie told me later that at one point, right before a big show with Bad Religion, with an audience of about 800 people or so, Al had come and said that Tré wasn't needed. Billie said, 'Well that's it! That's the last time that's going to happen. You're not going to come just barging in.' So from that moment on, Tré was the full time drummer and told everybody so. I think that it was hard on Al, too. He loved the band, but didn't want to commit his full time and energy to it at that point. So he went ahead with university and played in a garage band called the Ne'er Do Wells, along with a couple of other projects, and gradually receded from view. It's kind of a shame, because I think he played a really large part in Green Day becoming what they did. I think he's had a pretty happy life in the long run. He made a fair bit of money from the releases that he did play on, and the last time I saw him, he was happily married with a kid and making films in San Francisco, so I think he's doing okay. However, I do think he deserves a bit more recognition for his part in the Green Day story.

Q Just to backtrack a bit there, what was that first tour like?
The first tour, in the summer of 1990, was a completely DIY, punk-rock kind of a tour; I think Al probably organised most of

it. By this time, an informal network had sprung up thanks to the scene that was beginning to grow around the country. You could just phone up or write to people in a variety of cities and ask them to set up a local show at their club, or often in their house. A few bands had done this, like Operation Ivy, who were the first from our scene to come back with all these stories of what it was like out there, and how kids across America were starting to hear about our bands. So by the time Green Day tried it in June 1990, there was a warm trail that led across America. I remember, that summer I was staying in a university town - it was a very small town in northern California, the same one where Al went to study - and they started their tour there. They drove up from the bay area and came into town. The first show had kind of fallen through, so they had to play semi-acoustically in someone's apartment, and there were people shouting from the street, 'Shut up that noise!' That was the way those kinds of tours worked. You didn't know until you came into town whether it would be a fully fledged club with a professional sound system, or someone's basement; if there'd even be a working PA. Or if the police would shut it down, or somebody's parents would come in and say, 'All right, you've played long enough. Stop your noise!' The band made their way round the country like that, and I think they had a few equipment and vehicle breakdowns, but they survived. I know during that summer, while they were laid over in Minneapolis for a few days, they made another record, called the 'Sweet Children EP'. It was four songs that they had done way back in the beginning and had never recorded before. That led to a lot of confusion. Many people think to this day that that was their first record because it's their old songs and it's called Sweet Children. But its actually just something that was recorded in the middle of the tour in 1990 for a small label out in Minneapolis, and by the time they came back to the bay area in August they were conquering heroes. They were starting to draw a pretty big crowd back in the bay, and I'm sure at least a few hundred people came out to see their first show back. That was when Al dropped his bombshell.

Q Do they ever revisit the stuff that was on that EP?
Very rarely. In the early days, up until Dookie really, their shows were really diverse, and they would make up their sets as they went along. I've got a few recordings of live shows where they would ask the audience, 'What do you want to hear? Do you want to hear that one now? No, I don't feel like playing that... Well, okay I'll play that one.' So they'd dredge up all sorts of old chestnuts. However, later in their career they had a pretty formal set-list that tended toward the newer songs. I haven't heard any of those really old songs for quite a long time. There was a cover of The Who's 'My Generation' on the EP which they kept on doing for quite a while afterwards. I think that that song is a good fit for them, though, because they have a little bit of that sound. I think that Tré has become quite an admirer of Keith Moon over the years. I remember when they first started to break through, their first manager was apparently a buddy of Keith Moon's. They were sitting around celebrating the night that they got their first Gold record for Dookie, and their manager was telling stories about partying with Keith Moon. Tré was sitting there in the corner, wide-eyed and with his mouth hanging open. I think that Tré has carried on the spirit of Keith. Hopefully, not to the same extremes that Keith went to, but in the musical sense at least.

Q We spoke to a journalist who went out there and met them, and she said that the whole time Tré was just plying her with Hooch...
Tré is a very lively character, which is why I picked him for the band in the first place. He seems to have a certain immunity to

alcohol - and other substances - which other people don't, and he does seem to get delight out of trying to entice other people to join him, knowing that nobody's going to be able to keep up. I learned quite a few years ago to not even try.

Q What was the first thing that they cut with Tré?
The first thing that Tré worked on with them was during the autumn of 1991, about a year after he joined the band. In fact, they did a demo in the spring of '91 of five new songs, and I thought that they were ready to do an album. But they told me, 'Actually, that's all the songs we have.' So it was postponed, and then in the autumn of 1991 they went to in record what became Kerplunk.

Q What were those five songs on the demo?
I can't remember which ones specifically. There's some confusion, because Kerplunk only had 12 tracks originally. Both of those early albums were released on CD with bonus tracks - that was a punk thing in those days. It was considered immoral to put out a CD that could conceivably hold 73 minutes of music and only have 10 or 12 songs on it, so you had to pad it out with all sorts of other things. We reissued 39/Smooth on CD with both of the previous EP's and a bonus track included. Of course, later on, everybody bought CDs, and so they assumed that the album originally included all of those tracks. The real 39/Smooth is only 10 songs and the real Kerplunk is 12 songs, plus the Sweet Children EP tacked on to the end of it. This time I think they took about two or three days to record the album. I know that it cost about $1,500, as opposed to the first one, which cost $675. That reflects how fast they whipped through their sessions.

Q Why did it cost more then?
Well the second time they took a couple more days…

Q Why? I mean, is that because they were better, because they were allowed to, or...

Well, they were both. They were a little bit more serious, they were better, and they were certainly allowed to. After all, by that time, our record label was getting successful. It wasn't quite a shoestring operation anymore, and we could afford to spend one or two thousand dollars instead of only $500 or so. I think that they were starting to take themselves a little bit more seriously, musically, as well. I mean, it is still incredibly cheap, but on the contemporary punk scene, there was a caché attached to being able to do your record really fast and really cheap. Bands almost competed with each other, bragging, 'We did ours in three hours man', 'well ours only took two and a half.' In a way it's kind of cute, but in another way it's sad because some great bands only got a half-assed recording as a result. You can overdo things, as many mainstream bands do, but there's also such a thing as not giving it its due.

Q How did Kerplunk sound to you?

The first time I really had a chance to assess it was when I took the tape down to Los Angeles for mastering. We had a really good mastering guy down there. He'd been in the business 30-40 years, and I used to hear stories about him in the sixties working with Frank Zappa, the Beach Boys and Frank Sinatra. So, we started mastering the record, and as we went through it I was focussing on the components of the sounds rather than the overall picture. The mastering engineer made me a cassette of the album to listen to back home on ordinary speakers, not those giant studio speakers. So I put the cassette in my Walkman when I got on the plane back home to Oakland. Just as the plane was starting to taxi, the first chords of '2000 Light Years' kicked in. That was a scary feeling, it really was; I suddenly realised that this was something way bigger than I'd bargained for. By that time, my record label was paying its own way, but

it wasn't making a huge profit. I would've considered myself lucky if I'd just made a decent living with it. But as I listened to this album, I knew that everything had changed just like that. We'd already had some fairly decent success with Operation Ivy, and although they'd broken up, they were still selling great. Up until that moment I had no reason to believe that Green Day were going to become bigger than Operation Ivy. But there was something about that record; I just knew it was going to be big.

Q There wasn't a single released was there?
No, we didn't do that kind of things in those days. This was still a label that was being run out of my own living room, after all. I lived in a single, 12' x 12' room, and there were a couple of college kids that came in to help out. In the morning, I'd fold up my bedding, sling it in a corner and they'd start working; when they went home I'd sleep on the floor. That's the kind of professional offices we had. We just pressed up records, sent them out, and hoped that people would buy them. There was no marketing, there was virtually no advertising except for in a couple of punk fanzines, since our advertising budget was usually about $100 or $200. If people bought it, great, but if they didn't, well, try something different next time.

And yet, when that Green Day record came out in January of '92, it sold 10,000 copies the first day. We had never sold more than 2,000 records on a first pressing before, so it was quite a shock. And it just kept on selling.

Q Did you know what to do? Did you think it was inevitable that they were going to go to a big label?
I guess the transition happened gradually enough that we weren't running around like headless chickens, or in total shock. That came later, after another couple of years. But it was more like the grand plan unfolding! I never expected it to get too big, but my plan was to just leave it open-ended; to press as few or as

many records as people wanted to buy, and not to have too many expectations. When we sold 10,000 in one day, I just said, 'Oh well, I guess we've got to press some more.' I know that sounds silly, but it seemed like common sense, and that was what we did. Luckily, by then we'd hooked up with a really good independent distributor called Mordam Records, and they were able to get our records out there, and unlike most independent distributors, they actually paid us regularly and on time. It was a dream situation. We were very fortunate, and they made it possible for us to keep pressing records. Because we had always religiously paid our bills on time (This was my own blue collar, working class upbringing. My father did not believe in credit; you pay everything when it becomes due, you don't ever go into debt.), the pressing plants were happy to press records for us and trusted that we'd pay them. That's something that trips up a lot of independent labels when they suddenly get a demand - they just can't afford to pay for it. We were lucky that we grew fast, but not too fast, at least for that time. For most of the spring of '92, Green Day kept selling, and Operation Ivy, who were still our biggest seller at the time, kept on selling. The label kept on growing, even though it was still in my bedroom, and we were all having a great time. Green Day were playing more and more. They were touring, and they went over to Europe, and to the UK for the first time. I went over on one of the trips myself to see how things were going. They played the Railway Tavern in Euston station, The Pan Tiles in Tunbridge Wells, and on Christmas Eve they played some working men's club in Wigan where they notoriously re-enacted the birth of Jesus, with all of them playing parts. I guess that some people were scandalised, and other people were highly amused. On that tour through Europe and the UK, they were very much doing the grass roots/ DIY thing that they'd been doing in the USA in earlier years. It took a while to catch on, but it did eventually, and they built up an audience and toured as far out as Poland, almost to the Russian border. I remember going out there a few weeks later with a different band thinking, 'I betcha no East Bay punk rock band has ever been this far East, you know. We're practically in Russia!' and I look up at the water tower in this small town - it was called Bialystok, in eastern Poland - and there was 'Green Day' painted on the town water tower.

So they kept very busy, and I didn't see quite as much of them as I used to, because they were both in Europe and all around America. They were still doing their own tours, booking everything themselves, and about this time was that Tré's dad started driving them around. He had bought this old Bookmobile, a sort of truck-cum-bus that acts as a mobile library for remote areas. Tré's dad was quite a character; he's been on TV a few times. He resembles one of the guys from ZZ Top, with a long beard and a very boisterous manner. He must have been in his late 40s at the time, and probably having the time of his life, driving this young punk rock band around the country. Not too many young punk rock bands would want to go out on tour with one of their dads, but Tré loved it, they all did. Sometimes they'd come around to the 'headquarters', i.e., my front room, on a regular basis, probably two, three, four times a week just to hang out, ask questions, tell me how it was going and gossip about the other bands. When they were out on tour, however, I would go weeks without seeing them. But every time they played at Gilman it was still a really great night. They were also starting to play at bigger clubs around the Bay area, and the crowds were starting to come. I remember the first time I went to a show and couldn't get in, even though I was supposedly on the guest list, because it was sold out. At the time I was pretty indignant, but I also knew that things were changing.

Q That's terrible!
Oh it happens all the time, believe me.

Q You poor man.

I think that things continued in that vein all through '92. In '93 I was starting to think about doing a new record and we had some vague talks about it, but nothing really came of it. It was about that same time, maybe spring of '93, that the people around the scene who liked to gossip anyway, started coming to me and asking, 'What would you do if Green Day went to a major label?' or 'They're not going to stay with you are they? They're getting really popular.' It was the first I'd heard of it. I didn't have any reason to think they would leave, because as I said earlier, my idea of the label was that it was open-ended; it could be as small or as big as need be. Perhaps naively, I felt that we could grow as big as necessary to accommodate, however big the bands got. That being said, our scene was now getting enough attention that I knew there would be some interest from the big companies. One band from our area had already signed a major label contract with a subsidiary of Warner Brothers, and it hadn't come out too well. They'd made a record, spent a lot of money on it, and it'd bombed; they'd only sold about 1000 copies, when we could've sold a lot more than that ourselves. So I kind of took that as a cautionary tale. In fact, there was a whole lot of real hostility in the punk scene towards any band that went to a major label. Anytime a band did sign to a major label, there'd actually be picket lines outside their shows with placards calling them sell-outs, and that kind of thing. It's not an issue that came up a lot, and yet I knew it was a possibility. I guess it must've been late spring that somebody said to me that Green Day were talking to the major labels, and the next time I saw Tré, I asked him if there was any truth in it. He said, 'Well, why don't you get Billie and Mike down and we'll have a meeting', and so we all sat down at this local café. Within a few minutes it became clear that they were doing more than just talking; that they'd pretty much agreed to a deal with this management firm, a firm who were determined to get them a major label deal. So at that point there wasn't much I could do about it. My theory was, and I don't think it's a bad theory, at least in principle, was that they should do at least one more independent record before they signed to a major label. They had sold about 55,000 copies of each of their first two releases, which was pretty great for those days, but it was still little enough to get you dropped from most major labels. The big labels don't consider that amount worth bothering with, and I'd seen not only that one local band, Sweet Baby, but others too, who'd tried to make that leap too soon and ended up getting dropped. The whole experience was usually so disheartening for them, and they owed so much money, that they typically broke up. On the other hand, I thought that if some of these bands had put instead out another independent record, they were bound to sell at least 100,000 copies, and then they could write their own terms - the major labels would have to come to them rather than the bands pursuing the labels.

But Green Day felt confident that they could do it then; and in this particular case they were ready.

Q I suppose in hindsight they haven't ever really compromised have they? They seem to have been true to themselves. Would you agree with that?
Yes, they didn't have to compromise at all to get their deal. I think they were very fortunate, but I also think that they were very smart. They had a falling out with that first management firm later on, but whatever faults that firm might have had, they did get them a good deal. They were lucky to get hooked up with a guy at Warner/Reprise called Rob Cavallo who genuinely loved the band. I think that he loved them for much the same reasons as I did. He was a big Beatles fan so he saw the connection there, and he saw their potential. He told me, and he told the band that he didn't really want to change anything.

So the record label made no attempt (that I know of) to really change their sound, or to market them in any different way. I think the label just continued doing what I had done with them, but on a bigger scale: put them in a room, turned on the mics and let them go. So no, I don't think the band have ever had to do anything they didn't want to do. They've created their own path, and they've deserved what they've got.

Q Why was it called Kerplunk by the way?
I have no idea for sure, but I have a suspicion that it's probably more of their toilet humour, the same as Dookie - I assume you know what that one means?

Q There's a game in England called 'Kerplunk'. I didn't know if that was a US thing or not...
No, I expect it's probably - I may be completely wrongbut knowing them, it's probably the sound of a turd dropping into the toilet. That's the kind of the attitude they had.

Q What's a dookie?
It's American inner-city slang for shit.

Q What did you think about them re-recording some of the material from Kerplunk?
Part of the deal that we had with our bands was that, if they went on to a bigger label, they didn't just re-record the whole album, because obviously that wouldn't do us any favours, but it was quite all right if they re-recorded one or two songs. I guess they decided to re-record 'Welcome to Paradise' from Kerplunk for Dookie, their major label debut. 'Welcome to Paradise' is about this semi-squatted warehouse down in the ghetto of Oakland that they moved into when they first left their parents' homes. I guess that they were only about 18 at the time. It was a pretty rough neighbourhood; there were regular shootings and robberies all around. I went down there

sometimes for shows, and you could say that it was a poster for the American ghetto. Anyway, when they were recording Dookie, Tré came over one day and I said to him, 'For your first single and video, you really ought to do 'Welcome to Paradise', because that way you could have some social commentary. Maybe do some shots from the old neighbourhood and maybe have a message to your music.' One big criticism of Green Day at that time was that they were too poppy, just sang songs about girls, and were kind of fluffy. I told him, 'You could put paid to all that kind of criticism and you know, it's a really great song.' Tré sat there looking very thoughtful for a minute or two and said, 'Yeah, yeah, we could do that. That might be a good idea.' And then a second later, 'Nah, we'd rather drive a car into a swimming pool.'

So they ended up doing Longview instead, and I guess it kind of worked. Shows that I shouldn't be working for major labels and picking first singles. I guess they did eventually put it out as a single, but I don't know if there was ever a video for it.

I was walking down the Bayswater Road in London, after they played their first semi-big show there, at the Astoria 2 as it was called at that time. It was their first serious show in London, as opposed to the Railway pub and the other small gigs. I was walking back home along Bayswater Road when a van pulled up, and Tré was hanging out of the window. 'Larry, Larry, come on, do you want to come see our new video? I directed it.' I don't think that was completely true, but apparently it was based on his idea. It was the Basket Case video where they're all sitting in a hospital, and that was the first time I saw it; on the monitor in their van. All these years that I was doing record business stuff, I didn't even have a TV most of the time, let alone cable, so I'd never seen videos. We didn't deal in that kind of stuff, so it was all new to me. We didn't even move out of the front room until 1995. I mentioned earlier about us running round like headless chickens... That really happened in '94/'95 when Dookie took off, because almost instantly our old records took off too. We went from selling 10 or 20,000 a year to selling 10,000 or 20,000 a week, and suddenly we were a multi-million dollar business run out of this 12 x 12 room with three goofy guys and three telephones. When the management firms and the Warner Brothers reps came to visit us they were like, 'Where's your office?' And we'd reply, 'You're sitting in it!' There was barely room for anybody besides the three of us, let alone a whole band with their management and their A&R guy and their accountant. Eventually, in '95, we had to move into a proper office, which was exciting, but was also the end of the dream for me, in a way. Around that same time, I tried to rent another room down the street because it was no longer possible to live in my own room, but no-one wanted to rent me a place. The guy wanted to know my credit references, and I said, 'I've got this company, we're selling millions of records, and our office is up the street,' but the next day I came back and he said, 'Oh, I can't rent to you. I went to take a walk by your office and it's just some grotty old house. You're obviously making this up.' I had to go on living in my office for probably another year because nobody would believe that we were running this fabulously successful business from this run-down old hippy house on the edge of Berkeley town. But I got a kick out of that. It was two fingers up to the ruling class you know, 'We don't need you, and we don't need to do it your way.' When we moved into proper offices, with receptionists and phone answerers and all of that, the romance was gone, and I'd had enough after a couple more years.

Q Did they stay friendly with you?
They did. I saw quite a lot of them over the years, but I don't know what to say about it now because this is the longest I've gone without seeing anybody from the band. The last time I saw them was at Reading in 2004, just a matter of days before American Idiot came out. I went to the festival with them, stood on stage and watched them play to the fifty thousand people there. It was a really mental crowd; I'd never really seen it from that perspective. I'd been to Reading lots of times, but never before on the stage itself. It was a revealing experience. I'd never realised how big the stage is and how sterile and empty and cold it is up there; how the audience seems like they're miles away. It's almost like acting everything out in an aeroplane hanger. The band has to make every gesture bigger than life, and make it all really fabulously exciting, even though their audience are twenty feet away. They were, by this time of course, complete masters of their art - they just made it look effortless. Meanwhile, I stood there on stage shivering because it was a cold night, a typical English summer, just marvelling at what had happened. That was the last time I saw them. We hung out at the hotel for most of the night, and then they moved on with their tour. A few days later American Idiot came out

and exceeded all expectations. In my opinion it's probably their best record yet, and it made them superstars all over again. Things went even crazier than they did during Dookie, and I haven't seen them since that time, which is kind of sad. I miss hanging out with them, but it seems like they've entered a new order of stardom since then. Even though Dookie actually sold more records, for years after that you'd still see them hanging around Berkeley, turning up at shows, doing normal things; and now they don't seem to do much of that anymore. That makes it hard for me to say whether I'm close to them any longer or not, but it will be nice to see them again when I do.

Q Up until that point, had they changed? I always get the impression that they're the kind of guys that are nice and normal, but you know them, and you've always known them.

They haven't changed a lot. The whole thing probably it took its biggest toll on Billie, particularly the sudden stardom after Dookie. I mentioned earlier that I interviewed him about five years ago, about what had happened after Dookie, and he was quite shocked at how much hostility and rejection they got from the punks. Originally, the punks didn't want Green Day because they weren't punk enough, and now that they were big, the punks were saying, 'Oh you've sold out the scene.' They couldn't win one way or the other, and I think that Billie took that more to heart than the other two. Tré is just such a happy-go-lucky guy that he didn't really care what anybody thought. He was having a good time and he was going to continue having a good time. I think that Mike's a little more serious, but in a similar way to Tré, he's not going to be too bothered by what people think. Billie's a very sensitive and very thoughtful kind of person, and I think it took him several years to really adjust to the shock of stardom. But by the late 90s he was settled down. Green Day weren't as famous in the late nineties; their records weren't

144

selling nearly as much as they used to, and he had become a happily married father and was making a life for himself. I don't think they had changed all that much. They still liked to have a laugh, they were very funny guys to hang around with, gossip and make jokes with. I did notice that something seemed to change around the time leading up to American Idiot; they had become a lot more serious. Tré was still goofing around and so was Mike, but they seemed to become a lot more serious about their music and the way that it was presented. That may have been because of a period of declining record sales. It was as if they said to themselves, 'Well, enough of that. We're going to do something that's really great, because otherwise maybe it's all going to come to an end.' I noticed when I was riding out to the festival with them at Reading - it was almost kind of bothersome - they were talking to me as if I were the media or something. They were telling me all the stories about recording the album, stuff I'd already read in the papers, and at one point I said, 'Tré, I know you guys, you don't need to tell me all this stuff.' It was like they were, more than I'd seen before, playing a part. Not that it was a fake part, or that there was anything insincere about it. It was just that they were very much like other artists, actors, writers, etc. They had a job to do, a mission to accomplish, and very little was going to distract them from that. I also know that they were doing physical fitness training, so they were in the best shape, mentally and physically, that I'd ever seen them in; they had this real steely determination. Maybe they'd grown up in a way. Whatever it was, it seems to have worked in terms of making an absolutely classic record; at least that's my opinion of American Idiot.

Q Maybe they were kicked up the arse by their label…
I hadn't even thought of that. I'd so much admired their A&R guy and producer Rob Cavallo that I just never pictured him acting or talking like that. But I suppose that he could have…

Q You never know…

Well, if he said that then I'm sure he would've said it in a nice way.

Q I was just thinking about you mentioning them getting into shape, changing their image. That's all gurus, media advice isn't it?

I wondered at the time, as I was riding out with them, how this new record had generated so much excitement, when their last couple of records had just leaked out in a way. Especially the last one, Warning, which was such a low-key release. I remember thinking, 'I don't know if there's a marketing genius behind this, or if they're just in tune with the times,' but for some reason there was this incredible buzz about American Idiot. Until I heard it, I didn't have particularly high hopes for it, because I'd seen what had happened with Warning. The band had done what they wanted, tried some new experiments - they were worthy experiments, but they weren't experiments that the public seemed that interested in, so I was curious as to how American Idiot was going to suddenly turn things around. Like I say, they were all really on message with it; they knew what they were doing, and there was this relentless buzz building up. If there was some marketing genius behind it then they deserve a lot of credit. Of course, if it was the fact that they just put out a great record at the time, then that would just be pretty much how they'd always done things. It was probably a bit of both.

Q So now there are generations of kids who only know American Idiot; what would they hear if they put on Kerplunk?

To me it's pretty much the same band all the way through, and especially with that early stuff I hear real sincerity that's just genuinely heartfelt. It's three teenage kids singing their hearts out as only teenage kids can do. Perhaps they haven't yet learned to put on appearances, rather they're just so passionate about what they have to say and what they have to sing, and that's all that comes through. Interestingly enough, I've got a couple of young cousins who are big fans of American Idiot, so I made them some copies of the old stuff and they weren't that impressed. At the same time, I'm pleased to report that my 10 year old nephew has just discovered Green Day. It's kind of funny, because his friends were telling him, 'Oh, don't tell your uncle about Green Day, because it's not for adults, they wouldn't understand!' I guess my nephew found out from his parents that I knew something about Green Day and he came to me all wide-eyed and asked, 'Do you know Green Day?' I said, 'Well, yeah a little bit.' Then I made him a copy of their first couple of records and he was just over the moon. Maybe he's young enough to come into it with an open mind, whereas teenagers tend to think that if it's not on MTV, it's not worth listening to.

Q That's a very interesting point, I think you're right. He probably just gets the energy from it; it's pure energy.
Oh yes, he does. He and his friends just bounce around the room and sing along, rather like we did, back in the old days at Gilman Street.

Q Have you got any favourites among their catalogue?
For years my favourite record, and I would've told anybody, was 39/Smooth, their first album. It was just the right blend of songs and performance. Kerplunk was my second favourite and Dookie my third. I finally had to change that to American Idiot being my favourite, even though it's very slick and extremely well produced! I think it's just a classic album - it's not just a punk rock album, it's not just a pop album, it's one of those that'll we'll be hearing on oldies radio as long as there is oldies radio. Still, in terms of happy-go-lucky listening, I would still

pick 39/Smooth as my next favourite, just because it reminds me of what I originally saw that was great about the band. Kerplunk is a really great album too, but it's a little chillier. The songs are probably a bit better, but it's not quite as warm and encompassing. And I'd say something similar about Dookie; it's got some of their best songs ever, and best performances ever, and best production, but it's almost too perfect. I don't know, I've never listened to that record quite as much. Probably 90% of the people I know would rate Dookie as their best, but to me it's too good, and while I like it, it's the very newest and the very oldest that seem to be my favourites at the moment.

Q That's interesting. I think the drums are brilliant on American Idiot actually.
Well for somebody that saw that kid play drums for the very first time ever, I have to say that it's kind of scary to realise that I played in a band with this guy for five years. For the first year or so he could keep a beat, and that was about it. He was very hard to manage, especially at 12 years old, and it was hard work just to stop him banging on everything in sight! In fact, I used to take away most of the cymbals and just try to get him to play on the kick and the snare, and maybe a tom now and then. Within a year or two, I watched him turning into a pretty good drummer, and by 14 he was giving drum lessons to the other kids and playing in jazz bands and things like that at school. I think that now, undeniably, he's one of the greatest drummers in rock and roll. He can play all other kinds of music too, so if he ever decides to pursue a career in jazz or something else, I'm sure he would excel at that as well. It's just amazing to think of someone I've known since he was nine years old, when he was just a goofy little terror of a kid, and realise that he is that gifted… You're quite right, the drums on American Idiot are just mind boggling.

Q Do you miss those days when you were running your label?

For years I didn't miss them and I was glad to be out of it. Recently, I've been getting involved in a little local DIY punk scene in New York, and it brings back the memories. I did a festival last week in Baltimore where about 200 people came, which for this scene is a big audience. It was very much like Gilman Street in 1987; a bunch of bands that nobody had ever heard of, and a bunch of kids just going crazy. There was no commercial potential, at least not at this point, and no media recognition and that made me very nostalgic...and yet, why be nostalgic when it's happening right now?

INTERVIEW WITH
BEN MYERS

Respected rock journalist and recognised Green Day authority Ben Myers here gives a useful overview of the band's career, in this exclusive interview.

Q How do you view the band's first album, 39/Smooth?
Well, it was good enough for what it was at the time: three teenage boys making a racket. The production is kind of tinny and doesn't compare to the production they have now, but at the same time, the band were fully formed. Billie-Joe's songwriting was already of a pretty high standard, and they'd hit upon their own sound - fast and stripped down but melodic, with lots of harmonies and pop hooks. I think that that record, probably more than any of the others, owes something to sixties bands like The Kinks and The Who, and seventies punk bands like The Buzzcocks and The Dickies. It was recorded in a matter of days, so they worked quickly and you can tell. Taking that into account, it's still a pretty strong album really.

Q Does it suffer at all that Tré's not on it?
The first drummer brought quite a lot to the band actually. I think he, more than Billie-Joe and Mike, had ideas about production techniques. He wanted to work quickly. He knew that they were a punk band, and he knew that time was money. It was also in keeping with the spirit of what they were doing, which was something raw, energetic and teenage. Maybe his drumming was not quite as good as Tré Cool's was to become, but he was still young, and it was good enough basically.

Q How did Livermore's label work for them?
Well, the difference between being on an independent label and

a big label like Warner Brothers, who they signed to a few years later, was that they would be living a hand-to- mouth existence really. They didn't have much in the way of income, so when they weren't touring or playing shows they would have to do menial jobs, whatever they could. Most of the jobs were short lived because they would go back on tour again, but they did make some money by selling merchandise. They were quite astute when it came to that. They printed up t-shirts, and they had stencils or prints which they could take along. Kids would turn up at shows with their own t-shirts or shorts, and the band would just charge them for the print. Then, when they first started releasing records, they would carry a bunch of 7" singles with them, and sell them on tour. At that point, they would get a minimal amount for shows, but they would get enough to pay for their petrol to the next show. Gradually, because they toured so much, their records started selling, and as the records sold, Lookout were able to give them their share. But they weren't living on wages or retainers as big bands do now, and they wouldn't be given a huge advance to make a record either, they'd be given a few hundred dollars and told, 'There you are - go and make it.' It was after a couple of years of touring that the albums really started selling, to the point where each album had sold forty, fifty thousand copies each, which is quite a large amount for an independent punk band. At that point, the money was starting to come in so they could concentrate on the band full time, but they were by no means rich.

Q What was Kerplunk like?
Kerplunk, the second album, was really where Green Day came into their own. At this point they had been playing for three years. Tré Cool had just joined the band; they'd just toured with him and really refined what they were doing. Billie-Joe was finding his own voice as a songwriter. The big difference was that they'd moved out of their parents' houses and they no

longer had their parents' home cooking or anything like that to support them. Billie-Joe and Mike had been living together in a house with a bunch of other people, and I think that sense of freedom and independence came through in the music. 'Welcome To Paradise' was a song about being out in the world, leaving home, having no money, being mildly depressed about it but also having to get on with life. That all came through on the record. Equally importantly, the songs were stronger than they were on 39/Smooth - they were more melodic, more emotional; just more powerful. Again, the album was recorded quickly, but the production is slightly better and the songs are much better; that comes from touring for two or three years, they had a real bond there. Kerplunk was definitely a step up. It was the album that got passed around a lot in the UK, and that's when they started to make their name internationally, albeit in an underground way.

The band's first album had sold pretty well for an independent record, but at this point, punk bands got no recognition in Rolling Stone magazine, and MTV never broadcast them, because they didn't have the money to make the videos. Kerplunk was a strong enough record to break through without any kind of mainstream media presence, and it enabled the band to come to the UK and to Europe for the first time. I think it was October 1991 when they first came to Europe. They played sixty-five shows in three months, and it was quite a culture shock for them. The climate, for a start. When you're used to the California sunshine, a British winter is gonna be pretty jarring. They played squats in Denmark, in Germany, and then they went to Spain, just roughed it basically. They would play on bills with other punk bands, most of them obscure. They'd play with metal bands. They didn't get a lot of publicity out of it, but what they did in 1991 by touring Europe was start lots of little fires, if you like, across Europe, which when they came back were burning brighter. They built all these small followings in places like Wigan or Newport, came to London, played shows here and there. It's probably not recognised enough, but part of the reason that they became so huge worldwide was because they were able to go to all those different countries and do that. I think that the first European tour showed that they had a serious future as a band.

Q Why did they decide to sign to Reprise?
By 1993, the band had played four shows every week for three or four years. They'd sold fifty thousand of their first two albums each on Lookout Records. That was all that the major record companies needed to know really. They saw a band, and they might not understand the music, but they would look at the figures: here's a band selling fifty thousand records without MTV, without 'Spin' or 'Rolling Stone' or 'NME' or 'Kerrang!' At this point, they weren't getting written about, but still they had a huge following. They could go to Germany, England, France or Italy and there was a crowd there for them, so obviously the major labels started sniffing around, and once that happened, word spread. The band were just sitting at home in Berkeley, in their shared punk house, watching these A&R men pull up in their limos saying, 'You guys are awesome. We're gonna sign you. It's gonna be amazing. You're gonna be the biggest thing since whoever.' I think that they were used to a different world. They were used to eating burgers in truckstops and playing for beer money, so they had a cynical outlook to it all, which served them well. In the end they decided to sign with Reprise, which is part of Warner's, because they were impressed by their A&R man there, Rob Cavallo, who was a young guy who had already made a name for himself. He was also a producer and so he was able to offer that service as well. He turned up to see the band one day with a guitar and started jamming with them; they had a chat and realised that they shared the same outlook for

the future and the same musical reference points. Cavallo was able to say to the band that he wanted them to carry on what they were doing but with a bigger budget; make a really strong record, put it out there, see how it goes. Their expectations at that point were probably to sell a hundred thousand records, because even then, there were no big punk bands, not in the mainstream. It was really Green Day who started it all - they got so huge that they opened the floodgates for a lot of other bands. So at the tail end of 1993, they signed to Reprise.

Q What was the general feel and style of Dookie?
When the band made Dookie, they adopted a similar approach as they had to their early albums. It didn't take months and months to make, but this time they were able to use the best studios and take slightly more time. Obviously, there were slight pressures to get a record out. They didn't have major targets that they had to fulfil because they were a brand new band and Warner Brothers were taking a risk on them. The band's approach was quite relaxed and playful, although they've always had a strong work ethic. They had some new songs which they hadn't recorded but they'd been playing live, like 'When I Come Around' and 'Basketcase'. I think Cavallo was able to bring out the best in them, and nothing really changed musically; they didn't suddenly bring in an orchestra or extra musicians, it was really a case of just making the best record that they could. Three young kids with a following, a bit of money behind them and the world at their feet. They just went for it, and I think that the results spoke for themselves.

Q What impression did the first single 'Longview' make? I read that they just played it and played it again on MTV. Also, people talk about the post-Nirvana void and all this, I don't know if that's relevant to the success of 'Longview' ...
I think it is, yeah. By early 1994, things had come together nicely

for Green Day. They'd just finished their first major label record when Kurt Cobain died, and although the two aren't directly linked, because they were operating in different worlds, at the same time they were both major-label rock bands. Nirvana had been the figureheads of grunge, so from 1991 to 1994, grunge was what we got on the radio, and those were the kind of bands that got signed. Obviously it's quite pessimistic music on the whole: a lot of the bands capture the feeling of the time if you like. It's what people call Generation X music, which was loud, rooted in heavy metal, garage punk and hardcore punk. By 1994 it had dissipated and been diluted into just another mainstream rock form, so when Cobain died and Green Day came along, pop-punk was fresh. Both bands could be classed as punk bands, but Green Day were colourful and irreverent - they had fun, they had dyed hair - just the look alone was very different. Nirvana and Green Day were both outsider bands from similar backgrounds, but the main difference was that Green Day didn't take themselves quite so seriously. By 1994, when Dookie was released, I think that American rock music was ready for a big change. They wanted something more upbeat really, and it was the coming together of various things; the death of grunge, the rise of pop-punk, the slight change in the psyche of young music fans in America, that enabled the success of Dookie.

When Dookie was complete, Warner Brothers had a really strong album, full of potential hit singles. Green Day have been as much of a singles band as an albums band. They write really concise, neat, three-minute pop songs, and so the natural thing to do was to make some videos to show the world who Green Day were. All of the early videos, 'Basketcase', 'Longview', 'When I Come Around', were all pretty colourful, vibrant videos, but also straightforward, showing the band in their element, playing live. The record company were probably ecstatic 'cause they'd found a band with this really complete image that, while it wasn't really original, was newish at the time. Suddenly, within the space of three or four months, their videos were on MTV all the time, and the band was really visible because they were touring lots, their songs were on the radio and they were being played on MTV all the time. You know, you can't underestimate the power of television, particularly in America where the music press is more spread out and so has a narrower distribution. In the UK, you can get written about and often that's all it takes. In America it took MTV to get behind Green Day for them to become a household name, so they had these singles out. By the summer of 1994 they took a big step up and started playing on festival bills. They could walk down the street and people would say, 'That's that band that were on TV smashing things.'

Q Did this coincide with the festival circuit they did that year? Did the Woodstock thing really make an impact?
Yeah, that was the turning point I think, that summer. Suddenly there were these new bands coming out of the underground, bands like Green Day and The Offspring, who also appeared at this time - they'd been around for a good few years but they had just recently had their first crossover hits. Because of the backing of MTV, Green Day got offered bigger shows to do, and so in the summer they got invited onto the Lollapalooza tour, to play early on the bill, and they played half the tour. While that tour was going on, they got an offer to play Woodstock, the twenty fifth anniversary show. I think that the organisers of the festival were trying to recreate the spirit of the original Woodstock. Of course, the nineties were quite different to the late sixties and early seventies, things had changed. So Green Day were invited at the last minute to play Woodstock, and they actually flew in via helicopter. That was definitely a turning point, because they were given the whole rock star treatment. They were on a very mixed bill of bands. I think that the band before them was Peter Gabriel and his Womad collective, a bunch of

world music artistes, which is all well and good, but they were playing to a bunch of young, drunk, rowdy Americans who were waiting for Green Day. The weather was pretty appalling, it had been raining, and so when the band hit the stage it kicked off. Here were a band playing raw, aggressive music you could sing along to, and within minutes the mud started flying. The band encouraged people to throw mud at them, and it basically turned into a standoff between the band and the crowd, but in a playful anarchic way. Woodstock was being filmed and so this footage was on MTV straightaway. It made it to other news as well, broadcasts you know, and it was a defining moment in Green Day's early career. It was possibly Woodstock and Dookie in the summer of 1994 which cemented their status as this new, exciting young band who could inspire hundreds of thousands of people to go ape-shit and lose it. The stage was covered in mud, fights broke out between the band and security guards who were panicking, people jumped on stage. Mike

was tackled by a security guard who thought he was some kid from the crowd, and lost some of his teeth. It just kicked off big style, and suddenly they were the band that everyone was talking about.

Q Do you have any favourites from that period?
I think 'Basketcase' was the big single from Dookie. It was a massive hit in the States and a big hit in the UK as well. It is probably the band's most recognisable song, and up to 'Good Riddance' I think it was their most well-known single. Part of the reason for its popularity was that the lyrical tone summed up everything which Green Day sang about: dissatisfaction with life, confusion, doubt about the future, and there's usually a girl involved in there somewhere. The video for 'Basketcase' showed the band playing live in a mental asylum; they were trussed up in straitjackets, bouncing off padded walls, and it was really quite a simple approach for a simple song. It was on radio, and it was on MTV all the time for weeks.

Q Do you think that they spoke to thousands of disaffected teenagers? Do you think it was a matter of timing?
Rock and roll is generally youth music; for people in their teens or their twenties, and Nirvana had represented those people for a while, but inevitably, three years after Nirvana released Nevermind, grunge had become something else. Some pretty awful bands began selling millions in the name of grunge, but they were really just boring arena rock bands. Green Day went back to the roots if you like. There was an organic approach there, and they were part of a tradition of bands like The Clash and The Sex Pistols, The Ramones and The Buzzcocks. But they were also influenced by the eighties hardcore bands which Green Day grew up listening to, bands like Minor Threat who were very fast and aggressive. Green Day were a lot poppier and a lot more melodic than those bands, and therefore they

had twin appeal. They could appeal to punk kids who wanted a bit of melody, but they could also appeal to pop fans who wanted a bit of aggression. By 1994, the mood had shifted in music. Bands like The Offspring, Rancid, NOFX, Pennywise, they had all been doing their own thing for a few years, but it all came together in 1994 when the world at large recognised them, and the record companies, most importantly, recognised the commercial appeal and started cashing in on it. So it wasn't that there was a gap in the market beforehand, it was just that money was pumped into the scene for the first time, and there was scores of punk bands that got signed in 1994 or 1995 off the back of Green Day's success. It was Green Day, more than any of the other bands, who spoke to the teenagers most because they were the youngest of those bands and the fans could relate to them 'cause they were living the same lifestyles and had the same worries and doubts about being young and growing up in America.

I think that if you're a band making good records that get played, it doesn't take much to become controversial and notorious. Green Day had this reputation of being an anarchic, riotous band, partly down to their appearance at Woodstock, even though essentially they were nice guys with this strong work ethic. The average pop music fan will turn on the TV and see a band breaking their guitars, throwing mud or dropping their trousers and it'll be, 'Ooh, you know, this is, a bit naughty.' It doesn't take much to get recognised like that, so throughout 1994, the more the band played, the more explosive the shows became. By December, their reputation as a band to jump around and break stuff was sealed. At the end of the year, they were asked to play a free show in Boston. I think that the organisers expected about five thousand people to turn up, but this was the newest and biggest band of the year. Something like fifty thousand people turned out, and security was pretty lax and not very well organised. Rumour has it that some of the security guards were actually inmates at a local prison who'd been let out for the day and had been brought in to just keep an eye on the crowd, which just beggars belief really. The band came on stage; they didn't do anything out of the ordinary for them. They played their songs and the crowd reacted as they do. The promoters and organisers panicked and wanted to pull the plug. As soon as you do that it only makes things worse, so there were a lot of the fans on the rampage, and the band, by all accounts, loved it.

Q It was a bit of a tall order to expect the band to top the commercial success of Dookie...
Yeah. I think when a band enjoys this sudden surge in popularity and they're on all the magazine covers and on top of the charts, it's very difficult to better that. If you sell ten million records when you're twenty-two years old, then it's hard to know where to go from there, but Green Day did the right thing. They didn't really change anything, they just carried on doing what they'd been doing. But by the end of 1994, early 1995 there was pressure on them of a kind which hadn't been there when they made Dookie. The record label always knew that there was commercial promise, but Dookie had shown just how much potential there was. If you sell ten million records at ten dollars each, it's not difficult to work out the sums which are at play in this band's career. So when it was time to make Insomniac, there was pressure to get a record out pretty soon. A band's shelf life is very limited these days, and you have to do everything you can to stay up at the top, but it was inevitable that they would never equal Dookie with a follow-up album that was recorded really quickly. What they did do was make a record which appealed to the very same people who'd bought Dookie. Insomniac was a slightly darker album, in that, lyrically, there was a little edge of panic and nervousness to it. The band have

spoken about how they were doing speed at the time. The old favourite punk rock drug, cheap and nasty, speed gives you lots of energy, but also has a real downside to it when you come down. I think that these pressures, staying up all night writing new songs for an album which you had to have done in a matter of months, informed the content of Insomniac. Musically, it was still fast, and it was still dumb in places and smart in others, but crucially it had plenty of songs which could get played on the radio. It sold millions of copies and people judged it next to Dookie. It wasn't quite as huge a success, but for a young punk band it was still a massive album.

Q Were they happy with this one do you think?
I think they were pleased with the album. They were pleased with what it was musically and they were pleased with how it did. The only downside to it was, because it was doing well, people had an insatiable appetite for to see the band in concert. So they were sent off on tour for months and months and months, playing increasingly bigger venues, sports halls right across America, Canada, Europe, and consequently, a few months after Insomniac had been released, they were pretty tired. I think that they were pleased with the sales of the record, but mentally and physically they were pretty run down.

Q Is that then why they pulled out of their European tour in spring '96?
Yeah, I believe so.

Q Do you think it was that they were exhausted? Was it a tactical move to stem the damage they might do to their reputation?
When the band got signed in late 1993, they'd already been touring for a few years, and at that point, bands might be taking a step back, but Green Day never did that. They got signed to a major label, made a debut album which sold millions, toured

it and then recorded another album straightaway, which they immediately toured again. By the spring of 1996 they were all slightly lost, confused, tired, emotional, whatever. Their lives had become a series of sports halls, arenas and radio stations. They were being asked the same questions wherever they went; the same mundane stuff like 'How did you get your name?' or 'Tell us about being punk rock', and all of that gets on top of a band. It's also that these three guys were living on top of each other for months or years at a time. By spring of '96 they had girlfriends or were married, and Billie-Joe had a young son. I think at that point they saw that unless they put their foot down and made a decision which came from within the band and their management, the situation was just going to continue, and they were going to be on tour for the rest of their lives, playing shows every night. They would just be exhausted, so they made a decision to cancel the tour and go straight home. Looking back at it now, it was probably a decision which saved their career, because when a band has hit that level of success, and their second album does well, that's often when things often go wrong. Exhaustion kicks in, or the drink and drugs take precedence over the music. Green Day did the right thing. At the time, they obviously disappointed lots of fans, but I'm sure that anyone could see why they made the decision.

Q In what way did they stretch their talents on Nimrod? What was different about this album?
By the time Green Day made Nimrod they'd established themselves, they had a niche, they were known as the leaders of this new punk explosion, but I think that they were seen as quite a one-dimensional band to people beyond the punk scene. They were seen as a band who just wrote simple, straightforward songs, and so I think with Nimrod they tried to diversify slightly. People often talk about Nimrod as being the album which has other elements in there - there's a Ska song, there's

a hardcore song, there's some instrumental surf music, there's a brass section - but really, if you listen to the record now, it's still a Green Day record, and it's still a band writing punk pop songs. I think more than anything they were trying to keep themselves interested. Again, there was a pressure to release a record relatively quickly, but because they'd sold so many records already, they were able to step back a little bit and take their time. Commercially, Nimrod didn't quite reach the same heights as Dookie or Insomniac, but it was still a huge record. Reviews were very mixed, but it still sold millions, so they were obviously doing something right.

Q Was everybody happy with it? Did the punk community sneer at it or did they embrace it?
I think that the most significant thing about the album was the single 'Good Riddance'. It showed a completely different side to Green Day because it was this really sparse, acoustic song. The video just showed Billie-Joe and his guitar, sitting on a bed in an empty room and, for the first time, people could see that there was a classic singer-songwriter element to the music. Billie-Joe had been influenced by Bob Dylan and The Beatles, but also bands like The Replacements and Husker Dü, both of whom were seminal eighties punk bands with this other side to them as well. Green Day had already had three years of being criticised by the punk community, of being called sell-outs; a lot of people had turned their backs on Green Day. I think that 'Good Riddance' was perhaps the final straw for some people who thought, 'Well, this is just a kind of dull acoustic song.' But that song introduced them to so many new people, and it was another turning point in that, when it was released, the perception of the band changed. At that point it looked like their career could be going downhill if they carried on just doing these three minute punk-pop songs. 'Good Riddance' was huge. It was played at half-time at the Superbowl, it was played on the

final ever episode of Seinfeld, it was played over news footage of the funeral of a soldier who was killed in the first Iraq war. It was a song which took Green Day to every radio station in the country. This song was the song which suggested that they had major longevity, and were not just a throwaway pop band.

Early on in the band's career, they'd always joked that they would never 'do a Neil Young', as they put it, which of course meant unplugging their guitars and going acoustic. But they did. They were actually invited by Neil Young himself to take part in this annual show that he puts on, fundraising for a local school. They agreed, and it was the first time they'd played 'Good Riddance' live I believe. Up to that point they'd been a young rock and roll band, but when they did the performance for Neil Young, just by being associated with him suggested that they were now moving towards being a part of that American song-writing tradition of bands who had come out of the underground, bands like REM that came out of the alternative college thing and became credible songwriters. I'm not making a direct comparison, but you can see how the public and the critical perception of them changed. The press would now see a band who actually wrote quite introspective songs which worked with just a simple acoustic guitar.

Q How did the songs for Warning come about?
By the time the band came to record Warning they'd had quite a bit of time off. They'd been at home with their wives, their kids, you know, and there were a few marriages and divorces along the way. Warning was really very much Billie-Joe's album. He was probably making a concerted effort not to write another straightforward punk pop record, and he realised that for the band to achieve longevity, they would have to diversify slightly. I think that he also wanted to prove to himself that he could write these other types of songs, like Elvis Costello, who was from a punk/new wave background, but is now just

seen as a songwriter in his own right. I think that Warning was really a snapshot of Billie-Joe Armstrong's mindset at the time. There were still elements of confusion with the world and dissatisfaction with the government, and with the way that things were being run, but it wasn't an overtly political record... it was more concerned with personal politics. The band had sold so many records that they probably knew they could take a risk and make a downbeat, more acoustic leaning record, and even if it did turn out a failure, they would probably sell one or two million copies, and so they took that chance.

INTERVIEW WITH JOHN LUCASEY

John Lucasey, owner of Studio 880, where the band recorded their two most recent albums, picks up the story.

Q So, John, tell me about Green Day coming to record at your studios...
Green Day first came to the studio to record Warning, and they had such a wonderful experience that they came back.

Q What was it like during the Warning sessions?
The first time that they came in here I'd never met them, and they didn't know us; I was introduced to chaos, it was just insane. They were pure punks. There were lot of practical jokes, it was a mess, and we had a lot of fun.

Q Cool, and they've just been back for American Idiot haven't they?
Well, actually, the first time that they came back was when they recorded a couple of songs for International Super Hits ['Maria' and 'Poprocks & Coke']. We became good friends when they recorded Warning, and they would come down for rehearsals, any excuse really. It was just like home away from home; a few minutes from their house you know, get away from the wife and kids maybe...

Q Did they not do the last album here?
They did, yeah. Green Day came here and booked the studio, and they were here for 15 months, because the record wasn't written before they came in here, and Mike [Dirnt], the bassist of course, came in here every morning with his cup of coffee. He's an insomniac, and he's definitely a workaholic, so he

was here at eight or nine, before I got here (He had the keys to the building.). I asked, 'What the hell are you doing here?' He said, 'I'm screwing around with the song,' and that was the beginning of American Idiot. Between him and Tré and Billie, they booked the studio just to experiment, to find out what they needed to do as artists - and apparently they found out.

Q Would they sit around jamming all day? I heard that they had a few games that they would play…
A few games!

Q Yeah, yeah I mean…
It was chaos. The outside parking lot was a go-cart track; these things weren't just little pedal carts, they were serious. We had ten of them doing 30-35 mph in this small parking lot, with this course made out of cones. I mean, we had people going to the hospital! I was flipped over, you know, and we had the Vice

President of Warner Brothers' A&R department being flipped and almost run over. There were no rules out there.

Q Who was the best?
Actually, Billie-Joe was the best, and it really pissed me off, because I have a racing background. I think it was because he had a weight advantage, he was lighter. He was a phenomenal racer. At first he was a pussy, but then he learned, which really annoyed me and I had to resort to being violent. I welded these big, chrome bumpers on to my cart and it was a bit like demolition derby. I called it self-preservation.

Q Was their behaviour different to when they did Warning? I heard that they'd loosened up a bit and decided to have more fun... because they do work hard don't they?
They do. I think the reason why they're so successful is because they're so damned serious about their business. You know, musicians tend to think it's just all fun and glam for the most part, and then they get lucky, they have a hit, and then just sit back. With these guys it's the opposite. They're true punks, and they maintain that in their actions and how they behave but, in the same sense, they know what they're alive for and that's to be musicians, to be the greatest musicians they can. They feel that they have an obligation to their fans out there; to do the best they can do, so they're workaholics. They're very serious about their practice times, and they're very serious about their recording time. They have a lot of fun around it, but if somebody has an idea, it's 'Get off your fucking cart, get inside and let's do this.' It doesn't matter who says it, they just run in. They know what's comes first; they have their priorities right. As long as the ideas were flowing, the fun in between was just to freshen up their minds.

They were probably here two or three months before Rob [Cavallo] came here because they were getting their ideas down and just having a little bit of fun. When Rob came, from what I saw, he was pretty awe-struck by what was going on. Of course, Rob is a major talent, one of the top producers in the world, and Green Day are one of the top bands in the world. Yet they still managed to surprise each other, which was awesome - I've never seen a reaction like that. Rob decided that he was going to set up camp in Oakland and so he basically moved out here for months. It was amazing; the commitment was incredible to see.

Q Why do they like recording here, John?
It's a home to them; it's a funky kind of neighbourhood, it's got vibe. If you listen to American Idiot, they sing about this small town [on 'We're Coming Home Again'], Jingletown, which is a little 5-block area on the east side of Oakland. They also mention "the Mom's and the Brad's" [in 'Jesus Of Suburbia']. Brad was my studio manager, he was very much a mother-hen and he'd come in and shout, 'What the hell are you guys doing? You can't be writing on the goddamn walls!' In here, we don't treat people like rock stars; we just treat them like regular people. If I get pissed off, I let them know I'm pissed off, and if they get pissed off, they let me know too. If and when they spray paint on my walls, I'd spray paint on their cars - I mean it's open season! They don't feel like they're being catered for, and free punks don't like being catered for. Neither do any of the other musicians that come here, and I think that's why they're able to be creative.

Q That's interesting, I didn't realise that
American Idiot was so steeped in this place. It sounds to me like it wouldn't really have been possible anywhere else. You know, this is their home. They have the keys...

Q Tré gave you a guitar didn't he?
Mike gave me a guitar. He's just a real sweetheart of a guy;

they're all very genuine people. It was tough for me to see them go, and I'm sure that they were very comfortable here. I started off as a bassist and so Mike gave me one of his basses.

Q Do you think they'll come back?
Oh yeah.

Q That's great. So did you hear much of what was going on with the music? Did you hear the progression over those 15 months?
I remember them working on 'Boulevard of Broken Dreams'. I remember walking into the studio in the morning and Mike just said, 'You've gotta hear this song.' They played it for me, and I just couldn't get it out of my head. It was awesome. It was funny; I never imagined that that song would be played on the radio because I felt that it was so deep, and there's a lot of pretty shallow stuff out there.

Q That's cool. Did Billie do a lot of the writing 'round here?
Billie's always writing. I If he's playing outside and he gets an idea, he writes on your car. Billie doesn't stop. In fact I'm sure that he's writing right now. It doesn't matter if it's three o'clock in the morning, if he gets an idea, he's gonna write. That's just the way he is.

Q Have they dropped by since they've finished recording?
Once in while. They've been on tour for so long, but I still get little emails saying, 'I'm clearing out my garage, do you wanna come and pick some crap up?' or something. I'm the mother-hen, and they're very bad. Very bad boys.

Q Yeah, they've got a scribbling problem haven't they?
Yeah, they've got a scribbling problem. But I also have a temper problem so… I'll put holes in drums - I don't give a shit. I hid Tré's car one time, for three days. I got my revenge.

Q Did they take it well?

Oh yeah. I mean, what can they say? I love those guys and it's just all in fun, but you gotta keep people in check too. I've had TVs thrown off the roof at me, things like that; all sorts of nonsense, and I'll smile, I'll laugh. But they know, and they prepare themselves, because revenge will happen.

Q Were they like that when they did Warning as well?

Oh yeah. The TV incident happened during Warning. The thing that I most remember about those sessions occurred after they'd left. A couple of days after they'd packed their bags and said 'thank you', the lounge started to really reek something horrible, and the games room started to smell even worse. I was convinced that there were a whole herd of dead rats somewhere. Everybody who walked in wanted to throw up. So we spent two days looking. We're looking under the couches and everything like that, and then all of a sudden, one guy who was working with me at the time said, 'John, I think we gotta get these couches out of here. I think the rats are in 'em. Look, there's a hole.' Sure enough, there was a hole, but it looked like a real fine-cut hole. So we took the couches out, opened up the bottoms, and there were all these cold-cuts, potato salads and things like that in there. Next, we went into the games room and therewe found another fine-cut hole, about face height, and there were a couple of steaks in there. So I called Tré up - he was in Los Angeles at the time - and I said, "Hey, Tré. How're you doing?' And he replied, 'Hey, dude, what's going on?' 'I found your presents,' I said. They were just about to go on tour, and he said, 'Oh, you did? What presents?' So I said, 'Oh man, I was feeling kinda hungry. The meat and the cold cuts and everything were just the thing, and I wanted to thank you.' But he said, 'Oh, that wasn't aimed at you, man. You know we love you.; You see, there was a band due in after them, and I think that Green Day weren't really into them; the singer was a bit of a show-boat. So I said, 'Dude, I know that. That's why I got you a care package, but don't worry. I'm gonna leave it in your mailbox at your house. So you'll get it when you come back off tour.' He knew I could've screwed him, but I wouldn't have gone that far, because I thought it was pretty damn funny.

Q It's like a bloody sitcom isn't it!
That's nothing. Hell breaks loose every day, here. I'm just pulling shit out of the top of my head right now.

Q Do you think they loosened up a bit with American Idiot?
American Idiot was definitely from the heart; it was definitely what they were feeling at the time, and they made it into a hell of an album.

Q Why do you think it is so popular? Is it something in the way that they recorded it?
When Green Day recorded Warning, they did it pretty much how any other band would do it. They booked a certain amount of time, because they're under time constraints to get a record

done. How do you let yourself go when you're under time constraints? It can be very frustrating. The three guys together are closer than brothers, and of course they're going to disagree from time to time - which I never saw a lot of - but they watch each other's back like you wouldn't believe. When they came in here for American Idiot, it was different. Billie-Joe, Tré and Mike had had a long career, and it was time that they did an album how they felt it needed to be done. So they stayed, and didn't leave until it was right.

Q Did you say that they came back for International Superhits?
Yes. The band did come back for International Superhits, to record a couple of new songs. I believe that they were here on 9/11, so that was a weird day in the studio, in fact it was a weird month in the studio. They were very happy-go-lucky, and then one day… it was just a really hard thing for those guys to deal with.

Q Is that true that there is a dominatrix [on 'Misery' from Warning]?
Oh very, very true.

Q How did that come about?
Tré was online on the computer in the lounge. He's always looking at the weirdest things, and this particular time he was looking at dominatrix girls, and just kinda yukkin' it up. I was just sitting on the couch, and my intern, who had just been promoted to assistant engineer - he was a real young kid, kinda nervous - walked in and I say said, 'Hey, Tré, you should hire one of those dominatrix chics to beat the hell out of my intern, you know, if he wants an album credit." Tré said, 'Yeah! Dude, you're not gonna get a credit unless you take a beating like a man!' Our assistant, Tone is his name, thought he was kidding. Next day, in walked Mistress Simone, and she was

scary. Stilettos, tattoos, it was awesome; Tré was happy. Tone, on the other hand, was freaked out. He wanted to run out of the building, he wanted to throw up, he wanted to cry like a little girl. He will never admit to that, but that day he got his ass kicked. And it's on the front of that song.

Q Did they get loads of other musicians in for that song?
Tré plays the accordion. They all are multi-talented, but you know, I can't recall who else came in…

Q I understood that with Warning they wanted to put more sounds in, so they got more people to come into the live room, but I don't know if that's true or not. Do you remember people coming and going?
They had a Mariachi band at one point, and horn players, but you'd be surprised how much they do on their own: harmonicas, mandolins, farfisa organs and all sorts.

Q Do you know why they picked this place?
Their road manager worked at a music store in a town called Walnut Creek, California, and I had a little tiny project studio there. I would go in and buy guitars from him, and we'd talk about this little band he had, a little punk band. Anyway, he couldn't afford to record a demo, so I gave him free studio time, and they did this little record. Well, he went off to work for Green Day as a roadie, and I came to this building. A couple of years later, I heard that Green Day were thinking about doing another album, and searching for a studio. So I called my friend Bill. I knew that he was working for them at the time and I said, "Bill, can you ask the guys to come take a look at my studio?' He remembered my little studio from before and he said, "They're a major band. They need a real place to work.' I said, 'Bill, trust me, this place is different. It's big, it's very different. Bill, remember a long time ago I did you a favour? All I ask is you go to the guys and tell them, "Dudes, this dude did me a favour.

Would you just consider going checking out his place?"' Bill said, 'Okay, I'll do that. They're gonna say no.' I said, 'If they say no, that's cool, but I'm here in Oakland.' He called back about an hour later and said, 'Yeah John, they're gonna come by. Mind you, they're not gonna use it for recording, maybe someday down the road if they need a little demo place, or to rehearse or something like that.'

So the next day they came, and it was really strange seeing those guys I'd known off the TV walk in my studio, and they said, 'Wow, you've built a real studio here.' Next thing, we had Rob Cavallo and Allen Sides, who's the studio owner at Oceanway, come down here to check it out. And they said, 'Tell you what, they really want to record here. Why don't you do something with the hardwood floors, do a few little treatments here, and then we'll do the album here.' BAM!!! Right there I put that stuff in and it was awesome. And now, whenever I do any changes to this place, I think about those guys, because they really know their stuff and I trust them very much. If I do something major I'll call them up and say, 'Hey, what would you think if I did this?' So that's how I got them here.

Q What's it like then when they arrive? How long does it take to set up and for them to get into it all?
Well, between their crew and my crew we got shit down. It doesn't really take much. Their crew set up their rig every day and every night at some place, in some country, in some town. So, when they have to just go down the street and set up at the studio, it's no big deal. A lot of stuff comes in, we have a lot of room, so a lot of it gets put away until they really need it. But it's really smooth, and that's one of the things that is important to them. They show up, and then they're here to work.

Q How does it work? They just bring Rob in and they use your engineers do they?

Well, their engineers eventually turn into mine and visa versa. They have great taste for great engineering; whether they be a new, up-and-coming engineer or somebody who's an old seasoned pro. They don't care about credentials, they care about what sounds great and who's pulling the great sounds and has the best vibe. I think that's very important. A lot of bands are not open to a new talent. I think we have the best sound in the world here, but it's only as good, it's only as fresh-sounding, as somebody who has the right ideas or the right touch, and our engineers really have a talent for that.

Q Do they have any special requests for anything?
A lot of special requests for a lot of things. I couldn't even begin, but it's all within reason, and if I can't do it, or I don't want to, then it won't happen.

Q How does their method compare to other bands'?
When Green Day record here they don't have friends hanging around, because things don't get done like that. A lot of bands love to have their little crew, and that's a recipe for disaster. But with Green Day, if something needs to be done, no distractions, they're going to do it. If Billie has to work late, his wife will come by with his kids and they'll have a quick dinner here, but other than that it's pretty much business - and play - but their play is doing music. That's the funny thing. They work so goddamn hard doing music, and then they'll say, 'I need a break, let's go jam in the other room', 'cause they love it.

Q Do you think they're the hardest working band you've had here?
Green Day are the hardest working band I've ever seen, and I've seen a lot of bands.

ABOUT CODA BOOKS

Most Coda books are edited and endorsed by Emmy Award winning filmmaker and concert promoter Bob Carruthers. Over the last 20 years Bob has filmed and promoted tours, concerts and made documentaries all over Britain and Europe in venues ranging from Hammersmith Odeon to Murrayfield Stadium, with artists such as Bryan Adams, Spandau Ballet, Jethro Tull, Status Quo and Katherine Jenkins.

The 'Uncensored On the Record' series explores the careers of many of music's greatest legends, encompassing a wide range of genres including classic rock, pop, heavy metal, punk, country, classical and soul.

For more information visit **www.codabooks.com**.

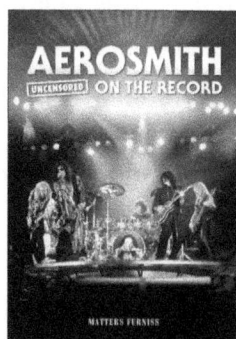

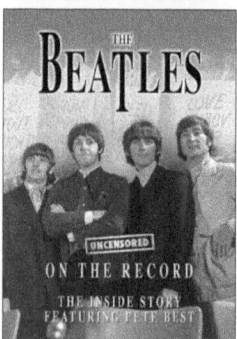

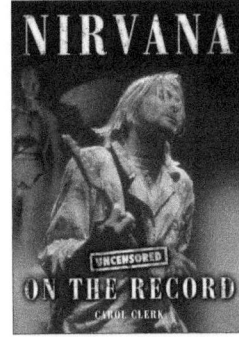

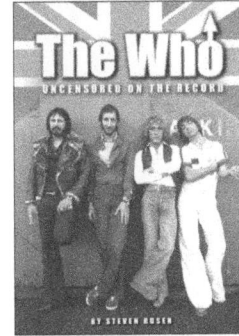